CRITICAL INTROSPECTION

Transforming the Internal

A. Sidat

Internal pandemonium

The mind-boggling external

Mental nourishment

CONTENTS

INTRODUCTION

Well, you've read the headings, and maybe you see the connection of this 'mental nonsense' or not yet. I say mental babble, or mental garbage, or mental fullness because the inner working of my mind somehow manages to consider a multitude of scenarios in a single moment (some of it unsuitable and undeniably unhelpful). As a result, all of it prevents any forward motion.

The knowledge of the right thing to do isn't clear cut. The attraction of the wrong thing doesn't necessarily instruct me to spring into this direction either (unless it's an escape measure. There's always an exception to the rule). There is a lack of reaction in both cases, but you'd think that at least one scenario/idea should ignite a fiery response. Could be fatigue, annoyance, past hurt, or a rut to explain this confusion and why sleep/bed/darkness has been a favourite pastime of safety. This mental fullness is a standstill of inaction and I was locked in its tight grip for too long.

Struggling with my mental health has been

an ongoing ordeal for many years. Alone in my grief, in my pain. Unusual methods of 'healing' were poor attempts at trying the wrong thing. In addition to trying too many things instead of embracing the wait so that peace could settle in. (In the end, there's just no choice, and these feelings you can't escape.) Other disasters included friendships with the wrong type of people. They subtly exuded pessimism and hopelessness, struggling with difficulties of their own. Had empathy gone wrong? I couldn't let them go, I was attached. To help another meant not helping myself, subsequently, the situation deteriorated.

How did it start? Or why? ... I'm unable to pinpoint to a specific time/place. If only it could be so easy, to get the answers to reach a satisfying explanation and close that chapter. But the mind is so very complex! The answer is a culmination of life's struggles, loss, and setbacks. The ineptitude of my ability to cope with the insurmountable rise of disaster after disaster. Shock after shock. Disappointment after disappointment. Let down after let down. Giving up is not conducive to healing. It's a state in which one continually reflects on those unchangeable circumstances (past and present). Although, it is helpful to look back and inwardly, to then look forward.

During my mental betterment journey (quest? pilgrimage? transition? hike? because it's strenuous until you reach the top/end, which makes it worthwhile? – sounds silly) I scoured several types of material to find answers about the Self. Leading me down a rabbit hole of: could it be hypersensitivity? Too much pain has made me soft as well as impatient (at the same time? How is that possible?)? Could it be PTSD? Absorbing too much from oppositional forces e.g. people, prejudice, hate, racism, Islamaphobia, discrimination, internal forces, or something else? Why is it always a plethora of things that bring about the end? This overwhelming pain that just adds to old, however, all pain remains fresh.

I was in this cycle of always surrendering to the pain, which meant never healing, never recovering, just a shadow of an unreal Self. I was done. Something internally switched one day. Could it be random? Something a human being cannot comprehend (i.e. there is more going on in the unseen than the seen)? Biological/chemical? Anyhow it drew me to writing as my chosen form of therapy. This method has always been beneficial to explore/air out my inner workings (a better term than 'inner-mess' which is critical and unhealthy). To shift from an absent, uncaring, devoid of emotion mental state, to a healthy one seemed a ridiculously impossible undertaking. But it was time to do something...

Experiencing challenges with our mental health links us to a group, but the strands within that group are so broad. It's impractical and impossible to generalise to such a degree given the nature of this book. Maybe with this route, you find something similar that helps you. Maybe by sharing methods we can help others? This exploration considers several internal and external perspectives. 'Compassion' means to bear in mind that more will be going on in the mind and life of another. We need this constant awareness before we speak, before we judge, before we assume! We need to be thoughtful, not careless with our words and behaviour. Maybe I could pass on a little spark of something, (as I've been asking myself, "What I have done for the Ummah/people?"). Self-reflection is a gateway to healing with faith at the foundation to steer us with purpose.

I'm worried about people, and the state of the world; the alarming rise of this mental health crisis, plus the suffering inflicted on people and on minorities all over the world. It tells me there is so much needing to be done. We are not here (living/being) without offering some assistance to someone, we need each other. You want to buy a house; you'll need an estate agent/realtor, solicitor/lawyer, mortgage advisor, surveyor, plumber, electrician, moving company/truck hire etc. You want to have a baby, think of all the people needed to make, deliver, and care for this child AND support the parent/s. Not just at birth but throughout these lives too e.g. dentists, therapists, teachers/educators, doctors, employers, customers, accountants, civil servants etc. We need people for their expertise, and what they can contribute to our lives, giving and taking (or paying). This system ought to make life easier and better. We can't do all on our own and we need help.

What is the bigger purpose of life? Why are we here? If we are on the constant lookout for ourselves how does it inspire or affect others? We further our desires, compulsions, ego, power, and obsessions by ignoring the essential and basic needs of many who are struggling all over the world. We need a balance somehow. Time for others (because this is their right over us), time for ourselves (self-care, to gain a better understanding of ourselves, time to reflect, to learn), and time for our Maker (the most meaningful, most important relationship).

Allah Azza Wa Jal (Mighty and the Majestic) is more than capable of giving ALL of us ALL that we need if we just ask with conviction, hope, and trust. I know that I am adept at nothing without His help and assistance. (I don't even have any control over my own heartbeat.) Everything I have, had, and will have is owed to Him, (praise be to Allah). After all, it all belongs to Him, including me. So we all get something, but it doesn't mean one person gets more so another gets less to have a balance as a whole. It's all an individual test at the end of the day (so it's a balance in our own lives). Our final fate is determined by Allah, the All-Enumerating, the Pardoner, the Giver of Justice. It comes down to our effort, belief, actions, intent, and above all our **heart**.

The purpose of this book is for you to honestly examine the internal. Be really candid with you, about you, and your behaviour, your attitude, your beliefs, your hang-ups, and your past. All the good and all the pain. In time, iron out a place that you are contented with, to maintain that internal equilibrium as best as you can. We can never plateau (in terms of deen/seeking knowledge) because it means we've become complacent, so we have to keep moving forward.

Life can be an agonisingly jarring expedition but this worldly life is NOT the last stop. Don't be drawn into the illusion. This is not our heaven (permanent happy), we're just passing through.

Follow me on this journey of admission and exploration…

THE MIND

Our minds are the gateway to our everyday living. How we perceive people, the daily struggles, and the challenges. Also how we approach/tackle problematic people, relationships, jobs, and chores etc. Our minds create the purpose or even lack of purpose. Do we have a reason to get up in the morning? Do we have a reason to make breakfast? Do we have a reason to keep or maintain the relationships with the people in our lives? How much do we control in our minds and to what end? What part is a conscious effort and what part is mindless repetitive action?

Is there a point to getting up? If so, what is it? What pushes you? What or who creates your reason to work hard; to go to work, to succeed in school/education or business? Do you have children, parents, or partners relying on you? Is this your purpose? Is it Allah Subhanahu Wa Ta'ala (may He be praised and exalted)? Faith? Is this your purpose?

What do you do when you lose your purpose

and your focus? The days meld into one. There is no day and night. It's just time, as a whole, fused into one nonstop action. It shifts into meaningless mechanical repetition. Sooner or later you may ask yourself, what is the purpose, what is the reason? If this is where you are, then what sort of questions have you been asking and are they the right type of questions of the Self? To what extent are you too engrossed in this life? Do these questions about the Self consider the future or the afterlife? Are you fulfilling your religious obligations? And if you don't know if you are, are you willing to learn, and change? People say life doesn't come with a manual… well, for Muslims, we have the Qur'an, and we have the sunnah of Prophet Muhammad صَلَّى ٱللّٰهُ عَلَيْهِ وَسَلَّمَ (Sallallaahu-Alayhi-Wa Sallam. Peace and Blessings of Allah be upon him).

The mind can be preoccupied with habitual awareness of the beauty in nature, and appreciation of the One who created it all. Or, it could be scrutinising the hopelessness, leading to frustration, even anger. If the days are blurring together with no significance, then how did we get there? How did it happen? Did we choose not to get up that one morning, not to do the dishes, have a shower, or allow the mess to pile up? Did the one day become four, a month, and now just routine life under the clouds? What mental fullness are you hoarding? What is this build-up of cluttered emotions, uninterrupted tears, and overwhelming fear? Are you losing yourself in the harmful perception of the problem? Has the conscious-ness stopped observing and analysing beyond the make-believe?

We are all struggling, whatever the cause, the reason, or the hurt. I've been struggling with my inability to focus, to sit in one place, to work when I know I need to. I can't think and focus on the task at hand for a multitude of reasons. Some-times its system overload because it's all the pain competing with the present. There is an endless list of everything waiting to be done, and all else I'd rather be doing. I then busy myself with phys-ical activities that require no mental exertion, I cook, I eat, I can do laundry. In addition to heedless tasks like watching 'nothing' (I'm not invested in it. I don't even care for it). This hollow entertain-ment dulls my internal racket.

Overwhelming ailing guilt follows, but it doesn't help to thrust me into action. What's my reasoning: "I'm doing something," "I'm satisfied at least one task can be ticked off my list." All dis-tractions prevent me from doing what I need to do (the real action – i.e. fulfilment, progression), keep-ing me numb. Even though I want to accomplish and do things, my mind freezes so that I'm unable to function. Yet I've been accused of "Being lazy," or "Lacking in ambition". I know I've been holding on to a lot, all crude statements about me declared as fact, subsequently internalised as truth. "You're too…" "You don't know how to…" "One of your weaknesses is…" And on, and on… Do you have any?

It's my mental state that has kept me stuck in a solidified loop of perpetual passivity disengaging from life, from people, and everything expected of a basic outdoor routine. Functioning just enough to get out of bed, dressed, and to work. But that wasn't always the case, prior periods of unemployment looked a lot worse, and I'm thankful to Allah Azza Wa Jal those days are behind me. Circumstances can play a huge impact on our mental health, e.g. our ability to cope, to proceed, to push. Or succumb and just sit in a state of lethargic idleness. In my case, a state of feeling under pressure but too weak and disheartened to perform.

The loss/deficit keeps me sitting where I am. I could sit for hours in one place, but my desire to write does not come.

Helpful thoughts do not materialise.

I'm not struggling with just one thing, it's an immense number of clawing things. Maybe it starts with the physical pain or the pain of the past, leading to doubt, to self-loathing, ending in apathy with little follow-through. Do I believe the naysayers, do I think it IS laziness?

The debilitating pain within us puts a stop to any chance of moving on or possible future fulfilment. Some demons survive so deeply within our minds that we wish it away. We wish for it to be over. We then spread some of the hurt with our bitterness. How we react in situations perpetuates our inability to progress by allowing the hurt to continue. For example, in a work setting, you may have a 'lazy' co-worker not pulling their weight. However, from the co-workers perspective, it's you who's the let-down. You've lost the edge. Is it possible that they are having an off day or several? Is it possible that you too have spent some time slacking off? Or have you been present and active 100% of the time?

We can spend excessive energy preoccupied with what our colleagues/family/friends/neighbours (and even celebrities) are or aren't doing. To what end are we fuelling these negative thoughts? All-consuming opinions about others can lead to rage/resentment/jealousy... which can develop into... regrettable actions.

Work has a massive impact on our mind. It's where we spend most of our waking day and most of our energy. It can be unpleasant and exhausting (to say the least), and the approach of employers/ teachers/educators (even the approach of families) can potentially worsen our mental health or repair it (e.g. self-esteem building by way of encouragement, and listening. Also giving the benefit of the doubt). A kind word, gratitude, appreciation, acknowledgement, gift, and thoughtful reciprocation can go a long way in just improving someone's attitude. Because an individual's life is more than just the relationship we have with them. Hold back on sarcasm, and observational comments. ("Oooh, you're wearing lipstick today." "Yeah, I knew you were Indian when we spoke on the phone." "You've got a healthy appetite." "You're in a good mood?!") People will misjudge your intent. Learn from your mistakes and the harm done unto you. Be willing to apologise, even if the intent was misunderstood.

If your mind is a tormenting cacophony of constantly passing judgment, creating an imaginative universe of another's life, ask yourself who has the power over that noise? Who has the power to control the judgement? Is this imaginative universe escalating, where a person's one off-day is catalogued so that it adds to other mistakes? In your mind, they become the villain; more useless, more destructive, and more irritating. Using one irregularity, on top of other accidental mistakes against them. What percentage of this imaginative universe is productive/useful, and for whom? Who are you alienating? What are you suppressing? What do you shy from addressing?

Sometimes the problem can be our own making, maybe because we choose to react harshly in a situation instead of pausing to think things through with a calm disposition. As a result, we cause harm and receive the same treatment, (not always, but people have limits, and usually dealing with something already overwhelming them). A blunt voice can be a harmful punch to an individual on the receiving end of the intentional hurt. Let them live as they choose.

Be careful with the control you exert over others as it can suppress and discourage.

Why is it important to let go and let them be? It builds relationships and respect between people. A sudden frank reaction will divide two parties rather than create harmony.

Do not be controlled by a mind which only expects perfection (perfect disposition/mood/attitude, agreement to all demands, following through with promises/chores/tasks), simultaneously expecting the worse due to feeling let down. This is also the case for a family (or people we live with) setting. Expectations lead to constant struggle, at some point we ought to realise that people do not fit into a box that we set with OUR forecast, limits, ideas, and knowledge. Why does it matter? Because it's cyclical neverending pain. Our compassionate nature ought to respect people's methods/ideas/approaches. Yes, we have to draw the line somewhere when it comes to hate

– and sometimes these haters just don't recognise this hate in them. Nevertheless, WE can work on our understanding of people. WE can work on our patient and composed temperament.

We will see progress in ourselves and our relationships if we can possess a calm and compassionate approach.

The Prophet صَلَّى ٱللّٰهُ عَلَيْهِ وَسَلَّم said, "The best of you are those who are best to their family." (Tirmidhi 3895). No doubt it can be testing and aggravating at times, especially the ego that compels: "I must say my piece". (I pray that our families do not become a test for us. That we all look deep within our selves with the intention to change for the better.) As Muslims, we need a regular reminder to ensure we are on the right track, not falling into old/bad/learnt behaviours. This happens when we stop looking inwardly and questioning the Self. We need to work on extinguishing suspicion and doubt in others. At the end of your day do you evaluate your encounters, conversations/words, actions, expectations, consumption, temperament, or prayer? What is the purpose of this exercise?

Keep doing good, and behave with kindness, mercy, and compassion. Why? Why is it important? We pass on our prejudice/hate/attitude when we don't act with kindness, mercy, and compassion. Or behave/act/respond without prior thought. We teach our children how to behave, how we talk/treat people, and how we address problems etc. They are always observing. Even if you don't say, "We need to talk to our elders with respect," they will view/examine/follow how WE talk to our parents, elders, partners, friends, or strangers. We might use profanity whilst driving or when talking about our issues, become easily irritable, or enraged in 'high-pressured' situations (this is subjective, different for each person). We may use aggression (through our behaviour/words. Even just a look can be intimidating) at the dinner table, or habitually express our displeasure at our circumstances/people. We may gossip, or watch/listen to inappropriate things in front of them. We may be careless with the food we eat (halal vs haraam), or express our aversion towards a certain group of people? All this and more our children, family, and outsiders see and learn from us. Did you behave appropriately? Or did you lose it, and say, "It was a fluke," or "It's not a big deal"? What impression do you give to people at home, the workplace, travelling, and beyond (including commentary on social media)?

Something I picked up from my dad is how he would talk to people. From a young age, I would go out shopping with him on the weekends. I used to love it because it was just me and dad without my brothers. He would let me pick a bag of sweets at the checkout, or something else while we were walking through the aisles. I felt guilty because he was working two/three jobs at one point, but he would insist. I think he quite liked me tagging along because he appreciated the help with packing, and I hope my company. At the checkout, he'd say with a big smile to the Cashier, "Good morning, how are you?" Sometimes he wouldn't get a response, but he'd carry on nattering away... "My wife needed these..." (depended on what we ran out of that week. Could be anything from frozen veg/fish fingers (as this was our typical Saturday lunch), butter, baking powder, or fruit). "We had to come to get my daughter..." (typically something sweet, any type of pastry/almond croissant/doughnut) then he'd wink at me. It was his way of saying 'I love you'.

Once the groceries were loaded into the bags and trolley, and we were about to leave he'd compliment the Cashier, expressing his gratitude (deserved or not deserved – we can't judge), thinking maybe they're having a tough day, or it was too early for talking. "Thank you so much for your help, Dear/young man. Have a great weekend/day." He was so forgiving and understanding with everyone, always giving people the benefit of the doubt. He told me how important it was that we put our best put forward and show good akhlaaq (character/manners/etiquette). What can you remember about your outings with your parents? What important messages/ideas/teachings did they impart throughout your life?

Our parents are the first (and most impressionable/ long-lasting) representation of what people are like, what relationships are like, and how people behave, react, judge, discuss etc.

My book of deeds is all about **my** actions, **my** wealth, **my** time, and **my** relationships. How did **I** behave? How did **I** treat people? How did **I** use what was given to me as a blessing from Allah Subhanahu Wa Ta'ala? If you're thinking, "I don't have any blessings, not a single one," start with the basics/obvious (although, I don't believe these are insignificant blessings. I say this because I know it would be devastating if the following were suddenly taken away – though we do learn to adjust eventually). For example, sight, hearing, taste, smell, functioning body/organs, health, read/write, speak, the nights you went to bed fed (happily, or unhappily due to your distaste). (I pray that for all who are facing difficulties, Allah Ta'ala grants you ease, comfort, and relief. Remove and protect you from all trials/tribulations.) The mind is controlling us, and the demon inside may push us to not concede, to not look inwardly and agree we make mistakes. Even prevent us from remembering all we've ever enjoyed.

The mind spends immeasurable time processing all memories. Re-evaluating, rearranging, and retracing to find meaning in our observations, in our lives, in our failures. Are we always correct, drawing only from what we know and our own experiences? We may need help to make sense of the memories, and perception of the memories, before placing judgements on people and the disaster. Which is why we need to talk it through with someone trustworthy. Gaining an outside view from a professional or a friend/family/spouse. It helps to do this in order to move on/move forward. Also for the eventuality of addressing an issue with an individual causing us trouble/distress.

There are darker forces at play some times, not always intended for your better well-being. There may be rogue thoughts in our consciousness. These demons in our mind can become so loud and so visceral. "Mum is this and that." "My co-worker was just robbed, ha. Well shame on them, they deserve it for being so rude." These demons create the single-mindedness; the noise to our everyday existence. In the end is it the demons pushing us, holding the key so we have no control over our own lives? If we are then powerless and keyless, what control do we hold over our future?

We cannot succeed and strive for more without control. The exhausting demon is a mammoth firework display of constant fog. Often it doesn't make sense. Bursts of trepidation. Whis-

pers of suspicion. Wave after wave of overwhelming anguish. Escalating hate. All of which linger
just to remind you the demon is near. You can't
think straight and you no longer hold any hope.
The emptiness of hope quickly occupies the mind
and becomes food for the demon, capitalising on
our suffering. It's not just another day now, it's
much better. It's a takeover.

Is all lost?

BREAKDOWN
OF THE MIND

The breakdown of the mind we never see coming because we give up a little here and a little there. Accept defeat a little here and a little there. Succumb to the numb void a little here and a little there. We become accustomed to the categories of loss (e.g. death, end of relationships/jobs, wealth, homes, health etc.) a little here and a little there. Ingest, inhale, and internalise the critics. It's a build-up of agonising emotion with no end in sight.

The breakdown of the mind we do not intend for it to happen, but it still happens all the same. How much does it happen to us? Or, is it that we lose the fight and daily struggle? Too often we say and have heard it said, "Well, that's life". It sounds like a heartless statement, but it demonstrates the lack of sovereignty we have over our circumstances and encounters. We have infinitesimal control over the good and the bad. Perhaps you're an artist, an engineer, a teacher, or a student still deciding on the path ahead. How often have you tried to succeed in something and seen it fail? How often do you push yourself, leading to sleepless nights and long days, to reach the finish line just to see the result fail? Too often we fail, and we fail, and we fail some more. "And that's life." Are we supposed to get used to it but not give up? How do you not give up? What does "That's life" mean?

You've tried time and time again without success. You've said to yourself it's hopeless. Wouldn't it be foolish to keep trying at something, not recognising that this endeavour was never meant to be successful? Ask yourself, is it the person pushing for more, or is it that the project has no merit and could never succeed (as a cynical Self, in addition to a pessimistic outsider would have us believe we will never progress)? Is it that the people of today do not see the worth of your work? Is it for them? Is it for you? Is it for Allah Azza Wa Jal? Are there some who could revere this piece of work to be more than it was perceived to be at the time of creation or publication? Does it mean that creation/effort has merit (depending on intent), but just the timing could make the difference between success and failure?

Time can change the perception of our struggles.
Time can change the perception of our success.

Our views, wants/desires adjust with time. And we can look back at our lives with a "What was I thinking" examination. Our observation of accomplishments and failures will mature and alter with us. If the ultimate aim is to please Allah Subhanahu Wa Ta'ala our success will never be determined by how others see us, or whether or not they accept us, or like our work, or if we receive a great big paycheck. Because when it is purely for Allah, we can achieve contentment in our hearts, for this reason, we can be at peace. As a result, by gathering strength from the Almighty, we will keep pushing: "Hold firmly to the rope of Allah." (Surah Ali-Imran 3:103). Such a powerful statement, with incredible depth. How does this ayah apply to daily life? How could it transform your outlook? How can this ayah engineer hope? (Take some time to think this over.)

Failure is only definitive if we terminate the inner and external push.

What percentage of people succeed in ALL their endeavours? Alternatively, how many projects can one person succeed in? Do we drive ourselves or do we have a team or support system in place? What do we do when we accept all failure to be, "Just life"? How do we encourage movement, without self-exploration? Once we allow the failure to be all we amount to then we are truly lost. Because the breakdown of the mind, is a breakdown of our internal push, a cessation of the fight (or even caring to fight), it becomes depression. The expectation and acceptance of failure we swallow far too easy and prematurely. What part does faith play during this crisis?

We lose hope in ourselves, in our talent, in the purpose of our everyday. Questioning it all in an instant, ready to throw in the towel. Rejection after rejection. Why did I fail? Perhaps seek out a friend for support and reassurance but never receive the right words you want to hear. Deep down we know people can disappoint us, or suddenly disappear when we need them. We question our talents and reasons. What did propel us no longer drives us because we take the loss, and the failure too personally and conclusively.

In the end, the closest person we have is just ourselves sometimes. We need to be able to rely on our Maker, the Possessor of Glory and Honour, and ourselves by working through a difficulty. But where is the energy concentrated during this loss? What role does Allah Azza Wa Jal have during our hopelessness if you can recall He is the One Who Removes All Difficulties, He is Just. We are not alone. We will always have Allah, the All-Provider, as long as we turn/return to Him humbled and with complete **trust**. Are you a believer when you need something? For example, getting into a car, embarking on a journey (du'a for travelling), going into surgery, applying for work/have an interview, have an exam followed by preparing for results day, having a baby, or you (or a loved one) are sick. How much time do you make/set aside for the One Who Gives Life? In a 24 hour day, how much of it is spent reading/reflecting/understanding/learning/memorising the Qur'an? Measure the level of importance you've placed on faith. Is there room for more?

Within this breakdown, we may also hold onto failure forming comparisons with others who've tasted success. How did they do it, how have they not felt failure? The truth of the matter is, of course they have. All human beings have felt failure in their lives. The comedian or artist would have spent years working from the ground up. Small gigs and small shows/exhibits that didn't make much, that were considered unsuccessful, possibly career-ending at the time. Maybe it felt like "Why bother?" Questioning, "Why am I doing this?" Have you ever achieved lower grades than you were expecting/hoping for? Have you ever baked a cake and it sunk in the middle, or baked some cookies and it expanded into one giant unappetising, inedible mess, even though you followed the instructions? (Sorry mum for wasting your ingredients. But making sure I wasn't too discouraged to try again.) Maybe you didn't get a job you wanted because you couldn't understand how a computer programme worked at the test (pre/post-interview), or you were having an off day, or you were just too nervous (my heart beats rapidly every time I recall this BAD interview). OR just didn't get the job and you don't know why, even with your attempts to get feedback. We see the success in others, not the failure that came before it. Preach success but not failure.

Our viewpoint is what makes us or breaks us.
Surveying it all in a negative light is
the beginning of the fall.

What if instead, you were to take some time to create a timeline and remind yourself of the rewarding struggles. Every effort that turned out to be an advantage, some admiration of Self, some accomplishment no matter how great or small. (The jobs you did get, the painting/product you did sell, the course you completed, passing your driving test on the fifth attempt.) Because they can still be categorised as an accomplishment. Will you see more failures or successes? Does it matter since you tried and made an effort? What if the narrative was altered, and how you perceive the failure is not as a failure at all. Instead, a successful attempt at learning what doesn't work. It could be the character deficit we need to work on (impatience, too cautious, fussy, inflexible, domineering etc), the route we need to change (job/career, education, city etc), or an unconventional direction we stumble upon unexpectedly.

If you believe in something through and through, pursue it. No matter the time it will take to accomplish or the people who choose to discourage. It is after all YOUR journey, not theirs. The ability to succeed can only be determined by you and Allah, the Fashioner of Shapes. If you intend to please and obey the Glorious, the Self-Sufficient you can never fail, no matter how the world perceives you. People will twist it, I know! But if we follow the Prophet's صَلَّى ٱللّٰهُ عَلَيْهِ وَسَلَّمَ example and sunnah, then how can we stray?

What causes you to stop questioning yourself, and reconsider a path? This wave of uncertainty can make us question why am I not perfect, why can I not fix this task/problem? Human beings are not perfect. Our bodies let us down sometimes. We feel too deeply, which can be crippling at times. We can be cut and hurt easily. A fall could leave us with broken bones, in bed for weeks. We face disease, chronic illness, even something contagious and viral could leave us bed-bound or suddenly gone. Our bodies may in some part be weak (AT TIMES), can the same be said for our minds? Bear in mind our bodies are resilient and can fight some infections. Even miraculously carry on some time after an amputation. Due to the willpower in trying to get better with physical therapy. So we're mortal, we know this. But we are also fighters, if we believe, then decide we can. You just need one person to believe in you, and that's YOU. Although it can be an asset when you have someone on your team, not everyone has this. What part does the breakdown play when we rely too much on others and not enough on Allah? Have you established a balance? With Allah Azza Wa Jal and the Prophet ﷺ in our hearts, in our lives, in our daily thoughts, we can never be bereft.

The Almighty has given each of us
gifts, skills, and talents.
What are yours?

Who is in control and who holds the key to our breakdown, either as a vortex in or as a ladder out? Well, the demon within/around us takes over, occupying all thoughts which brings us to a place of self-pity and self-sabotage. A destructive nature ensues. Depression for some could be dealing with the problematic ordeal of simply living day-to-day. Depression for some may be part of our makeup, something that needs maintenance with regular checks. Perhaps taking medication and/or therapy is the answer or an exploration of other avenues to deal and cope. Whether it's leaning more heavily on the Knower of Subtleties (securing and maintaining this daily connection – which we all need to do), exploring types of therapy, exercise, or socialising in some way, there is an acceptance of living in the now while working on letting go of all that has past.

You are an inspiration.
There's a story to tell overcoming those battles.
You have accumulated wisdom, self-control,
and spectacular fortitude.
Were there moments in your past you
didn't think you would move on from,
that seemed/felt neverending?

The breakdown of our minds may be a poor reaction to the struggle. An inept system to deal with tragedies, or unable to compromise settling into a new perspective. How much of the past are you holding on to? And why? "School bullies criticised anything and everything about me. My clothes were too short for my height. My inability to hit a ball, and successfully take part in any physical education was a reason for ridicule." We deal/ swallow this harsh treatment regularly. Then we pile on additional suffering by holding on instead of releasing.

Oppressors/bullies will cause harm to others, with consequences like suicide to the one they inflict pain upon. When did people decide the actions of this life were unanswerable in relation to the bigger picture i.e. the afterlife. Do we choose to believe words and actions are unseen so that we can live a free life? False invincibility can lead to immoral actions, which is why Muslims are meant to fear Allah Azza Wa Jal. It's not so that it paralyses us, its to keep us on the straight path, to be fair, honest, responsible, and kind to all. A reminder that we are accountable, that Allah is watching us. There is always a price to pay, whether we choose to believe in the One Who Has the Power to Create Again or not. Be mindful of your words, that joke, that sarcastic remark, that cruel underhand observation.

I know the past hurts. I'm not saying it doesn't, or that it's not significant. But how much of this past are you holding on to, and why? What is the barrier preventing you from transcending beyond this affliction? How does the pain affect your day-to-day? How does it affect your relationships? How much time has passed? Are you ready to move? You alone get to decide. No human being can push us no matter how much they try or want us to. This is an internal momentum that can only originate from us, with as much determined fervour and resolute effort that we can establish and increase upon. What type of foundation do you need to move forward? I know we want to progress and try, but sometimes we still can't push, so...

"Ya Allah, please heal us and comfort us.
Eliminate the worries and troubles in our lives.
Grant us what we need inside to get better, and
achieve. Help us to pick up and keep moving. Gift us
with the best of this life, and the best of the next."

All I can say is keep asking for help. It's coming, and you have to believe it. You just have to! "Hold firmly to the rope of Allah," He is our strength. Don't let go.

Sometimes this past hurt is caused by the people in our lives. Try to look beyond what you see in them e.g. the actions you admire and dislike. Your perspective may not necessarily be an accurate assessment of these people, but it is an example of attributes in yourself that could need work. And to ensure we do not retaliate with this same treatment: e.g. rage, greed/miserliness, discourteous behaviour, patronising attitude, inconsiderate disposition. On the other hand, they may have attributes you admire to amplify: e.g. patience, helpfulness, warm/kind disposition, confident/encouraging attitude, generosity.

Look at past examples within a religious context at the people who exude mercy, patience, humility, and generosity. Dig into the history of the Prophet صَلَّى ٱللَّهُ عَلَيْهِ وَسَلَّم , so much care, consideration, empathy, wisdom, fairness, and thought for others. When you see hate voiced against someone, ask yourself what is their agenda, and where does this hate stem from? Because his life (صَلَّى ٱللَّٰهُ عَلَيْهِ وَسَلَّمَ) is an example to us. The rising hate in the world is worrying! Hate divides! Hate creates more pain! You don't want to be responsible for the breakdown and agony in another. All will be brought to justice, no stone unturned, no word/action/carelessness missed or lost.

Take some time to think about what is the breakdown of the mind. Why do I succumb to the negativity of others, why does it influence me so, why do I invite it in to examine it? Do you pick apart the hate, and allow the aggression forced on you to implode and to destroy? Whether it's a need to be liked and accepted, or not to rock the boat, being agreeable/ignoring may be a way to gain some distance and keep the peace. In some cases, the argument isn't worth the energy, people will form their condemnatory opinions of you before they even hear you speak. Their hostility and suspiciousness reflecting poorly on them, not you.

We cannot allow hate to pierce us, not only to wound but to have us respond in a deprecating attitude in kind. That is not you! Even if they take some time to get to know you, does it matter? Once the well of friendship/relationships has been poisoned, it cannot be remedied. We will never know what is truly inside the minds and hearts of another. Being courteous and careful with our words has to work both ways and if you aren't repaid the same civil treatment, walk away. Do not harm. Just walk away.

We must protect our hearts and minds.
Please be careful with your words, we already
know they leave bite marks.

It's necessary to frequently survey the people we have in our lives. What sort of people do we want and are they worth the energy and effort? How much energy/time/effort/love do they leech (expect) from me? Does this person allow me time with my Lord? How do they influence me, my mind, and disposition? What type of person am I when I'm with them? Do we encourage each other to be better Muslims, better people?

From a religious perspective, some relationships you cannot break and this can be a source of discomfort in a contentious relationship. Ask yourself what would Allah, the All Observing Witness want/expect me to do here? Is this act pleasing to Allah? Will it help me to get closer to Allah, or further away? What is the right thing to do? It may not feel clear cut but you are capable of figuring it out and finding peace with your answer. You'll know if it's right once you've established a daily connection with the Source of All-Goodness. If you've thought it through, Allah Subhanahu Wa Ta'ala will know your intent, so be mindful it's the right choice.

Some people may be easier to let go of than others. You may ask, do I care what they feel towards me, do I want to address it? Do I want to have a confrontational discourse? What does it matter if they form some hypercritical opinions, do you need to correct them? I do not need to accept another person's opinion of me unless I think it to be true. Maybe they think studying to become a teacher isn't an appropriate career choice. Should their disapproval and rejection rock my world and send me down a downward spiral? Do I want to change this about myself? Am I uncertain about my dreams? Express certainty in your aspirations/goals/intentions politely, and walk away with your individuality intact. We need more cheerleaders, more positivity. (Just be aware of how your mind and heart react to praise.) We can figure it out (with Allah Ta'ala) because we are capable. Or we can ask for help to get to the destination of our choosing.

The noticeable disapproval in others can be earth-shattering. Blow after blow, to attack and injure. The interactions we have with people can play a part in the breakdown. The things they say can eat away at us for years to come. Reliving and replaying in our minds. So again, please be mindful of your tongue. And only voice your observations if a loved one has genuinely asked you for help. Because they aren't changing for you, to please you, or to be a mirrored version of you. It will be to please Allah. Be gentle.

Our mental health needs treatment just as our physical health. The medicine will differ from person to person but a holistic approach will be needed to tackle all. My own mental health I grapple with regularly to ensure there is healing in each day to keep the demons from torturing me. These demons want me ruined so that I want nothing, do nothing, and care about nothing. Dealing with it means doing my best to ensure the mistakes are never repeated. It means detaching from the pain, subsequently altering my view of it. A new outlook with an unconventional spin (digging for the silver lining) will allow me to move on. Trauma can never be forgotten or erased, but the Supreme Solver can heal and alleviate this agony. We are consequently capable of moving on with time, which cannot be rushed or pushed.

New methods and new approaches teach us to be patient and self-analyse. Dealing with it means accepting our limitations and remembering the progress we've made. Contemplating all that just is, not make-believe; not tomorrow, not yesterday, but just is today. Focusing on the things within our control/effort/responsibility. Not those which aren't as they can cause undeserved distress. The data of our past can be enlightening. Enriching our present with deep regard for human life. We are capable of compassion and this is really what we need to possess and exhibit. For our sanity, and the sanity of everyone else in this world that we share, let's work on empathy and less dialogue of the garbage variety. What type of dialogue is fruitless, empty, and meaningless? Why is it important? Because it affects our hearts. Hardness vs softness. What do we ingest that make our hearts hard or soft?

We can (or we cannot) choose to influence our thoughts. It starts with us. Slowly working on self-analysis begins with a thought, building towards an irrefutable strong sense of Self. Make a choice. Allah Subhanahu Wa Ta'ala Exercises Responsibility Over All Things. There is a way out. We need to persist in order to reach our full potential.

THE THOUGHT PATTERN

The thought pattern is an initial automatic reflex to situations, people, and even empty space i.e. time alone with the Self. Our attitude to the information at hand (i.e. the challenge/worry) will be dictated by our natural thought pattern and analysis of data. The way we are so inherently inclined to assume, judge, and react, is a normal everyday occurrence. Whether it's from an analytical point of view to formulate an agreeable result (e.g. at work, driving, writing an essay, the solution to a problem etc), or to just look down upon like gossipping due to our prejudices/hate/unhappiness of the world.

A positive thought process could take into consideration the ramifications of words, actions, behaviours (is it appropriate?). How can it influence/shape this person? Am I responding because I'm annoyed, or because I have some 'valid' ideas about this subject? An instinctive adverse reaction in a strenuous situation when we're feeling over-whelmed, in addition to the lack of thought and patience could be disastrous for us and others.

The thought pattern may be troubled and perplexed: 'How do I combat this problem?' Are we capable of dealing with it and if so how? Taking into account past relationships and situations. How did I deal with a similar problem then, what was the outcome? Assessing the problem from various angles is a means to plan for an ideal resolution. When obstacles strike how do I initially react? How do I cope? What are the coping mechanisms I use to fight the stressful situation? Asking questions like, "Why is this happening to me?" is not a hands-on attitude, it will not im-prove the situation. It is indicative of anticipated hostility coming our way due to the outlook of our everyday. The addition of this fresh superflu-ous grievance could be capsizing as we react disas-trously without thought.

As a Muslim, I believe that Allah the Most Kind, will not burden me with more than I can bear (Surah Baqarah 2:286). However, in heavy lonesome moments of despair, my thoughts were all painstakingly obsessed with the unfair en-titled view of: "Why me?" "Not again!" A harmful repetitive cycle of all-consuming thoughts which prematurely wrongfully assume. These thoughts erupt, smothering any possibility of peace or way out. What are your initial thoughts to unexpected complications? I realise now it's ingratitude in the face of all I have ever had, achieved, and gained. This was due to my primary focus being on the catastrophic situation I was in. If I were to compare my hurt to the horror in the world around me (e.g. the injustices, the wars, famine, natural disasters, the unfathomable pain), I concede that yes it could be worse. This evaluation ought to provide me with comfort and gratitude (and soften my heart to help and reach out to others).

The thought pattern surrounding a problem is not succinct it's convoluted, it's a mind map, on another, and another. The threads and connections are seemingly endless. Because the rational thought pattern will take into account all past trauma, all awareness, and decide a cause of action or even lack of action.

I know it sounds impossible and unattainable to have hope. Or live with hope, or believe in hoping, or believe anything will improve or get better. I've been in a hole for years just barely getting by. If like a former version of me, you can come up with a hundred reasons to give up, I want you to find and focus on just one that can evolve, grow, and flourish. Our thought process is limitless once you get started in any direction (pros or cons – positive or negative). Do you see it? Try it out now on a piece of paper.

*By being encompassed in a concrete unshakeable
mindset we have a chance at defeating the
depression. We can conquer the naysayers,
and destroy the negative thoughts, not
only to survive but be victorious.
What fixed idea/notion will help you to overcome?*

At times our thoughts may be a poor response because our innate tools of coping can lose their potency due to our inner critical views. It can damage our mental health further. We do have to take a chance sometimes and we can't always know what an individual's intentions are towards us. Or what an outcome might be e.g. starting a new job, moving to a new city, exploring a new relationship/project/endeavour. If the thoughts you are internalising paint you in a negative light, then it is not helpful. It is useless because we can't move forward and accept those failures or mishaps as extinct in the past. This I've found leads to crushing emotions, as pain does not lie dormant but conscious and alive in the present. Life doesn't feel like one worth living when the agony can choke and cripple. Are you familiar with debilitating pain? I hope never to relive it, so I'm fighting as best as I can now.

Is the thought pattern struggling to swallow just the one hurdle, because you've reached your tolerance; retaining all past catastrophic complications?

ALL are dealing with something, which should make us more sympathetic, patient and knowledgeable in offering help if we can. For example, offering a meal to a homeless person because you know what it's like to be hungry/homeless/down on your luck/unemployed. You've had a period in your life where food was scarce/limited. You've experienced hardship and remember when someone/stranger offered unexpected help. The thought pattern can look back fondly or unhappily at the past. "I'm doing better today. Praise be to Allah. I'm grateful." Depending on where we are with healing (or the pain) e.g. attached/detached/semi-detached, it can shape our outlook of the present and the future.

Seeing a homeless person should act as a reminder to me to make a better effort to help. Make the time, because there'll be every excuse under the sun not to. Rushing here and there, no change/cash, no time, don't feel like it, having a bad day, in a bad mood, don't see/acknowledge them as people. Some people keenly express these harsh, and critical opinions. "It's their fault they're in this mess".

*People are watching us, and every word, action/
behaviour, kind/unkind gesture will be a part
(memory/stamp) in their story forever.*

Try not to react with annoyance if you're
feeling stretched and asked to do more. Consider
that with all the pain in the world, if I don't internalise a little and think about how I am impacting/
affecting other people, then my world is a selfish
one. I ought to look at myself first! As my mum
says, "There's always room for improvement". My
understanding is: do not be so arrogant to think
you know everything. Sure, you know a little bit
about several things, but there is someone else out
there who knows more and another who knows
differently. Be amenable to keep learning and ex-
emplifying. Be willing and open to working on the
Self, to please Allah Azza Wa Jal.

There's always room for improvement.
There's always room to try harder. There's always
room to do a little more. Does anything come to
mind for yourself? It all comes down to whether or
not you are so affected by something that it tugs
at your heart to change. Maybe it means working
on you, and maybe it means wanting to have an
impact on a larger scale. At the end of the day, it's
all for Allah Subhanahu Wa Ta'ala, and He knows
our intent and the condition of our heart. Don't let
the demon taint the intention, making the action

wasted. Being mindful of Allah watching over us can influence us to change. Being aware of suffering can educate us to be more considerate, tolerant people.

There are surprising miracles/potential/opportunities that arise when the blessings of the All-Giving come your way through a single act of charity. So why don't we do it more often? Or regularly? Alleviate someone else's pain while working on our own. Intention to do good will inevitably bring good, just don't expect it. Sometimes it's a lot and sometimes it's a little, and sometimes in this life and sometimes only in the next. The tides can turn if our days aren't spent in neglectful action, in service of the Self and only the Self.

You may think, well I have more pain than him/her, so why should I care? Comparing pain is not a competition. And what do you get if people concede your pain holds more weight than another? It doesn't make us feel better (unless it's some kind of ego boost). Do we mention it to vent, or to hold this title of: 'My life sucks the most'? It's not helpful to compare unless the act of comparison provides new tools in dealing with a problem. Has one person dealt with their struggles by communicating with the person causing the internal uneasiness? Attempted a different approach than your own? Or tackled an issue by moving far from the problem. Perhaps they've accepted that sometimes people won't change therefore ending a toxic relationship. Allah, the Hinderer, the One

With an Exalted Position Sees All, and since this life is a test for all types of trials, will I pass the exam? Passing the test brings awareness to the lives I helped, wounded or ignored.

The act of comparison as a method of 'They have it better' is damaging and uselessly time-wasting. We are all on individual journeys where our strengths and weaknesses lie in exclusive experiences and perspectives. Faith and goals differ us, siblings/parents/family impact us, their emotions and attitudes influence our outlook. Relationships will teach us what we are prepared to compromise and the red flags we cannot accommodate. My red flags will differ from another's, due to my tolerance and experiences. I may be willing to marry a divorcee or widower, or someone with children from a previous relationship. Whereas another may not want any of these things. Therefore, how could the act of comparing one person's progress, life choices, or pain to another compared with yours be useful?

If I'm in a state of wallowing I need to turn to Allah Subhanahu Wa Ta'ala in this and every situation. Refusing to turn off those unenthusiastic thoughts means I will continue in this stumbling cycle. We can work hard, but without asking for help from Allah, the All-Excellent, the Fashioner of Shapes, our endeavours will never succeed without His aid. Did you ever give up asking Allah Ta'ala for help? Why? What is your relationship like with our Maker now? How much trust (and effort in your du'as/prayers) do you put in Him fixing/healing, helping/alleviating your hurdles and issues?

An act of comparison with your own self could be prolific. Have you ever done this before? I compare myself to where I was five years ago; I'm not in the same place I was, I have overcome and achieved in some aspects of my life, (no matter how small). Even if I'm currently at a low point (no matter the cause) I know in time I can get through this, just as I have previously done. By comparing where I was, to where I am now. Comparing what I have overcome and endured. "I was well before, I will be well again." "I had a job before, I'll get a job again." I am grateful, forever indebted to the All-Perfect, for having aided and provided for me along this journey. My eyes are opening each day.

No day is wasted if we've spent it in the remembrance of the Magnificent One. No day is empty, by turning our thoughts into multiplying gratitudes. No day is without hope, so long as we concentrate on the now, and the circumstances/action within our control.

Allah Azza Wa Jal doesn't expect perfection from us, but we are expected to keep trying, never giving up, and absolutely never losing hope (as the demon would have us believe otherwise). "Hold firmly to the rope of Allah," He is your lifeline, the One Who loves to hear you call on Him. He is with you always.

RECOGNISING THE THOUGHT PATTERN

A deeper dive

Does your thought pattern develop negativity? What themes/ideas/scenarios escalate, and to what end? Firstly, we need to pinpoint where do our thoughts wander to? Secondly, what is the catalyst, the trigger and the harm of an unhelpful imagination? We can't manage our thought trajectory until we understand it.

We all have an immediate response, can you identify yours? For some, an immediate response may be to withdraw from a challenge/hurdle/unexpected difficulty. A group may react negatively with violent outbursts instead of thinking first. Feelings can become fact if we do not recognise/explore the internal. A self-fulfilling prophecy asserts our claims of: "All people are…" or "This accident will happen," or "It never works out." Others may not register the challenge as a threat and let it go, contemplating an alternative path fixated on a solution. What is your thought trajectory? How do unhealthy thinking patterns in our mental universe set impossible standards? Does your self-critique extend to an evaluation of others as well? To what degree/extent do you pick apart the Self – to flourish/empower/elevate or to crush/deflate?

Is your automatic response causing you to react pessimistically or confidently to difficult circumstances? How do we facilitate an alternative way of thinking if you think there is nothing wrong with verbally/physically abusing someone because they won't behave in the way that you decide? Or you habitually assume they are immoral/inadequate based on age, gender, race, religion, socio-economic background, education, values, ideas etc. Everyone's thinking pattern is dissimilar to yours. So why are we critically responding with immediate exhaustion? We are all brought up with different teachings, ethics, politeness/etiquette, faith/spirituality, circumstances/opportunities, privilege and on and on…

We all approach tasks differently. For example, clean the floor first before wiping the worktops. However, you decide it's wrong because you prefer to sweep last and wipe first. This means you sweep the fallen crumbs. One person sweeps before cooking, and another prefers to sweep after, and some will do neither. The person with clashing approaches to you undoubtedly had a different upbringing to you and this is the system they were taught. It could also be that they just like to do things in their own way, (as you may have learnt growing up with siblings/guardians/parents). Similarly, these are jobs/tasks they aren't bothered/uptight about, and it's not as important to them as it is to you. What habits in others are you unable to let go of? What subjects must you be outspoken in? Where does it stem from? How does it affect your relationships? How does it affect your health?

Yes, people can irritate us at times, if we feel strongly about a subject and force our opinion on them, unwilling to compromise or walk away. Can you establish why you are adamant about a specific topic, just as your opponent may be adamant their ideas are normal? Are there some trivial subjects, tasks, or styles you've reacted to poorly and if so why? There's always some reason we fixate on a particular annoyance. "I told you already, put the dishes back in order of size then colour?" "The dishwasher isn't organised this way. Do I have to everything myself?" Why is it so important? Control disguised as organisation. "No. No. No! Can't you hear? I said..." Rising temper followed by rebuking creates enmity, leading to resentment, and silencing. ("Do you want to keep your job?" "In my house...") It accelerates the breakdown of a relationship. Realistically there are only a limited number of chances a person can give before we accept, understand, and move on.

There are some instances where people in authority demonstrate little care. They do not appropriately address concerns from those who are struggling. The approach we take (in voicing our concerns – and our attitude to those provoking our temper/resolve) has an impact on whether or not our needs are met. Employers/managers need people training: empathy training, mental health training, compassionate training. But it has to go both ways and employees also need to think about how their behaviour affects their colleagues. Kindness is needed all around, not division. Why is it important? People are suffering! What does it matter if they are of a different race, religion, gender, age etc? What does it matter if they do things another way?

Recognise your thought pattern in all situations and know your triggers. For example, when your anger inflates (triggered by an individual's approach/method being different to yours) why is it eliciting a controlling nature in you? Why does their system matter, if the work is completed? Expressing your impatience may contribute to their lack of willingness to help later on, but also forgive your incessant nagging. More importantly, it could be detrimental to their mental health. Imagine they're dealing with: loss, grief, anxiety, or depression, and your frustrated intimidating attitude/response/remark is a step too far. Remember, we don't share all/any of our pain, and the difficulty we may be in.

We are responsible and accountable for our actions. Show care, patience, and compassion. Work on letting the trivial go. Be more complimentary and forgiving, instead of taking a hard-line approach with no explanation. "I really appreciate your help, and I just wanted to say thank you, I noticed." Or "I don't want to hear it. I've given you the list. I expect..." Which method will provide more fruitful results?

Instead of reflecting on our thought pattern (and temperament), we decide to inhibit another person's individuality. They will not be able to grow, as a result, neither will we.

Some subjects we deem mighty important and others not. At times we will talk to an individual, who cannot be reasoned with. They won't budge even with facts or just to keep the peace. "Please wear a mask, we hold all life dear and want to protect you ALL." A reasonable request to some, but arousing agitation and abuse from others.

Where has society, education/parenting/ teaching gone wrong? Where does all this hate and aggression stem from? Are we overworked and overwhelmed with life that we feel constantly under pressure and annoyed? Are we all pushing ourselves too far? What are we enduring and not addressing? Why do we not have peace in our hearts and lives? Do I care how my words or behaviour affect people?

In order to achieve peace, I realise I must be willing to ignore and let go of the inessential. What are the areas/ideas/expectations/topics you need to ignore to find peace? As you would expect, there are some situations which will call for an uncomfortable exchange. But only when I'm able to respond with clear post-thought, rather than a limited hasty reciprocation. Which would likely be harmful and crude.

Arguing/observing conflict/expecting abuse is a cause of anxiety. We may try our best to keep an argument from escalating, but we can only do this by recognising why our thoughts are pushing us to quarrel. An unconventional direction could bring harmony by ensuring we are steady with patience, love, compassion, and forgiveness regardless of the antagonistic attitudes in people around us. Why is it important? It shows your self-restraint and compassion. Don't get sucked in! It's brutal to keep quiet at times, even when you feel you're in the right. (Although the ego could be pushing me to believe I'm right and exert my control over others. I must check myself and my intent first).

Your opponent may be inflexible, and there can be no room for discourse if we are unable to think of the greater good. Where is the grey area?

Are you clear on what is right and wrong? We have religious teachings, and practices, this is our guide. If you feel unsure, you need to question yourself, you need to learn about Islam. What is your internal and external rhetoric? What is the message you are putting out into the world? Do you disregard the right action/deed/response due to circumstance, a rough day, prejudice, or due to a compelling/justified need to retaliate? Wear a mask or don't? Understand the need to protect you and all?

Recognise your thought pattern when listening to a friend's dilemma. Do you listen first, followed by offering suggestions that you decide are appropriate by gathering data from your own experiences? If having faced a similar hurdle (in your opinion), then clearly your advice must hold some weight. Human beings in our nature will try to be helpful to others (yes, there'll be the odd selfish duck). Whether the support is for a child, family member, neighbour, friend, colleague, or even a stranger in need, we will try to offer some comfort or assistance. On the other hand, some will put another person down to express themselves. Bludgeoning them with an outlook until they concede. Without the agreement of the recipient, who are we helping? Is it about control? Ego? I've heard a problem, so let's fix and move on, end of discussion?

Ask yourself if your approach is to talk at but not listen. It can bring a relationship to a halt since one parties opinion is deemed more valid than the other. The listener becomes aware of their silenced position. If the conversation centres on acknowledging a child's emotions (not turning them away), and being encouraged to explore solutions, it will build their self-esteem. Particularly for the eventuality of being on their own, for instance: at school, at work, and in all relationships where they will need to communicate and speak up for themselves. Their points may not always be factual or valid, but educating with an open-minded approach with love and nurturing (truly grasping their personality and mental state) will have a far better ripple effect. It will influence how they treat people, their siblings and parents.

There are many ways we can offer assistance without offering advice. For example, offer to call a friend once a day (or as often as they need within the boundaries of what you can give), arrange a walk once a week, or visit a relative with them. Maybe you know they aren't working so you give a little cash, whatever you can spare. And/or make some meals for them, because they're sick or grieving. As was the sunnah of the Prophet صَلَّى ٱللَّهُ عَلَيْهِ وَسَلَّم which was to send food to people who were grieving so that it lessens their burden of preparing food. Being a helping hand is crucial in aiding recovery while our loved one is aware of the effort required on their part to get better. (Always exhibit patience and hold your tongue if you get frustrated at their lack of change.) An anxious mind needs differing support from person to person, but to feel loved and cared for will sink in eventually.

Ask yourself in the moment, "What is the underlying message?" "What emotions can I identify in their choice of words and body language?" "How do my words/behaviour impact them?" Ask how you can help, because your method of encouraging them will not be received well if they don't want to hear it. You could offer advice they aren't interested in taking on board. You could even take the bullying hard-line approach which would alienate and wound. On the other hand, maybe it's what they want to hear, they don't mind this tactic? Does that sound right? Everyone is different, do you see how we can't know how to proceed if we do not know what people want/need. All you can do is ask how you can help. Above all, DO NOT lose your temper or show irritation/impatience. If someone is already in pain, this attack (because this is how they'll see it) could be a breaking point.

Consider that even if another person may think and claim they know what's best, you do not fit into a mould of their ideals. You will always get to decide the amount of effort you put in. On the one hand, is it advantageous to see it from their point of view, do they mean well? Are their suggestions better than what you could have thought for yourself? If that's the case then think it through as you will need to execute the plan, living through the hurdles and struggle. Try to be open and receptive. On the other hand, If you're not in the head-space to listen then vocalise politely. Ask yourself if you are feeling pressured in this new course or way of thinking. We all have clashing opinions/advice (one likes strawberry-filled doughnuts, one loves custard. One hates ALL doughnuts! One adores watermelon, one is allergic to all fruit. One frequently discusses politics, one prefers religion. One is quiet, one verbose), doesn't mean they are agreeable/suitable to you, or your path.

Recognising someone's motivations and the logic behind their approach will be difficult to surmise, however, be sure of your own. We must respectfully reject these ideas unless the solution is something we want. If you're feeling unsure or uncomfortable in a moment where opinions aren't your own, then say so. As hard as it may be to express out loud, a quick agreeable response without any forethought could be harmful in the long run. Sometimes it's better to be straightforward and tell people what you need. "I need to be alone." "I need quiet." "I need fresh air, can we go for a drive?" "I'm not ready to go back to work." "I need some time to think about this." "I'm not ready to talk about this." "I'm struggling."

The people in our lives will want us to pick up immediately due to their lack of understanding and displeasure: "Loss of potential." "Wasting away." "You could do so much." They cannot comprehend what it means to shut off and turn people away. If they aren't open to listening, that sometimes (for some people) suffering with anxiety/depression/mental health means needing time alone (not time away from them specifically) it tells you they have something to learn. And they won't get it until it's explained.

Although it's hard to put another person's feelings above our own in our overwhelming state, we need to try not to inflict any harm. Respond with gentleness, explain with reasons/consequences. As we are more aware of what pain can do, we can be sure not to repeat this cycle of harm. Don't ignore them.

Even though some people expect an instantaneous optimistic response to a setback I realise it's better for my mental health to take some time to be introspective and unleash my pain to Allah, the Caretaker. But this I've only learned with time. It helps to release the ache and explore answers/solutions. Due to this self-exploration, I can rework the vantage point as a beneficial measure to capture the moment. Deciding on a different course of action, when it feels right. However, to have change/opinions/suggestions forced on anyone without real thought to them, how their mind works (internal conundrum/overwhelmed senses), and the issues they're facing (internal and external) will not be impactful. This type of 'help' will never inspire a stable change. Being grateful, where we look for the silver lining takes time (because we may have been in a negative spin for years). Remember this ayah: "If you are grateful, I will certainly give you more." (Surah Ibrahim 14:7). What are you grateful for right now? Make a list. Thank Allah Ta'ala.

Permanent change occurs from within.
This internal drive will thrust us because we
have decided on a path we refuse to alter.
Allah Azza Wa Jal will guide us to keep us steadfast.

From a religious perspective, I realise how valuable it is to internalise and exude optimism and gratitude. In some cases and some situations, it just takes a little time while we sit with our emotions processing the day/hurt/loss. But I'm working on getting better at this. We aren't expected to get back to a normal routine or an instantaneous improved mental state after a loved one passes, it will be a slow process of healing (patience is key in these moments). Sometimes we can put pressure on people by expecting immediate transformation and turn to prayer. At the end of the day, if you're a believer we know where we are going to end up. As long as we have this in mind, then we know we have to try, never surrendering. So keep really trying. And yes, people may judge you for your efforts, even so, let's not judge them for theirs. Try to look for the silver lining even if the external is challenging. Why? It's pleasing to our Creator. "Help is always near," (Surah Baqarah 2:214), an ayah which sparks hope.

Your relationship with the Creator is unique,
which only you can know and understand.
The All-Hearing knows every single thought,
every single tear, every single experience, every
single relationship, every single regret/mistake
you've ever had/done. So talk to Him.
No one will understand us better
than Allah Azza Wa Jal.

No one can force you to pray, except that they're concerned for the state of your afterlife so take it as such. They're worried about us, so how can we flip this? "Please pray for me to get better." Ask yourself, do I want to get better? Do you recognise the steps needed in connecting with The One? Do you recognise your thoughts when it comes to the discussion of faith? Do you react in anger? Is this due to the approach of the individual/s pushing you to pray, or do you hold resentment towards the One Who Gives Life? How do you feel about the Most Compassionate? What do you think 'most' and 'compassionate' mean?

For an outsider (living, helping, or know someone with a mental health condition) please do not overwhelm their senses. If you hear, "Ok" with a sombre/dejected tone, or "Thank you, but I'm at my limit right now," or "I get it," maybe a little irritatedly (I'm not saying this is justified) because you won't cease with pushing, or you get a "Thanks" with no discussion, then STOP. We can either show you our true selves because you allow us to express and confide in you (which will not happen overnight), or we can hide away in secret where we explore dark and much more damaging avenues of help. Why? Because we learn we have no one and our circle becomes smaller and smaller. We realise we do not have someone patient enough to listen and care, judgement and commentary free.

Throwing positivity, and even analysis in the face of anxiety at its peak is redundant since we are not in that moment able to absorb/ comprehend/face/add any more than what our bodies are inundating us with. I am unable to see beyond the pain when all I feel is an internal flood of bubbling overflowing senselessness.

Recognising the thought pattern of pessimism and internal antipathy is an indication of what to address and action. The how on the other hand (putting a stop to it, or divert it) will take some time through self-analysis and therapy. And again, what will work for one person will not work for another. Prayer, confiding in the Supporter of All gives me hope. I repeat, "In the Name of Allah, the Most Compassionate, the Most Merciful." "Allah is enough for me (us), and the best disposer of affairs," (Ali-Imran 3:173-174) to eliminate the torrent of worries. Do you have an ayah (verse from the Qur'an) that is meaningful to you? When I break this sentence down and internalise it, this is what I understand (but know that I'm no Qur'an expert):

1. I need to believe inside (unwaveringly, concretely, completely) Allah Subhanahu Wa Ta'ala is enough for me.
2. I must acknowledge, and understand, and comprehend that Allah is Most High. Most Powerful. Nothing and no one is above Allah Azza Wa Jal.
3. I trust in Allah to have the best plan suited for me, even if I don't know it, or understand it. He is All-Knowing. He has **All-Encompassing** knowledge.
4. I accept Allah is Most-Wise. I know nothing. He is the Creator after all (Glory be to Allah). He is All-Perfect, All-Excellent, the One Un-

equalled, the Everlasting.

5. There is a way out from this difficult situation because Allah will correct my affairs, give me a solution, and a satisfying end. Because He is Most-Loving, He is our Caretaker.

6. I draw strength, comfort, and courage (the ability to carry on) from this ayah.

7. I realise that I have to hold on. I have to be patient.

8. Gratitude refocuses my mind, building my fortitude.

9. I must accept the decree of Allah Subhanahu Wa Ta'ala. This will help me to move forward. And lessen the strain on my heart when anxiety attacks my senses.

Making decisions pushes my anxiety to its limit so I turn to the One Who Guides in my drowning anxious state to give me strength. Life is all about making decisions: "Where should I study?" "What should I study?" "What path do I want to take?" "Should I stay in this job or move?" Including relationships: "Is this person right for me?" "What are his/her intentions?" It's important to recognise your thought pattern for different situations. "Do I want to approach this positively?" "Is it worth giving this person the benefit of the doubt?" "Can I live with this person, should I make

the effort to get to know them and compromise our differences and idiosyncrasies?" Anticipate
that we will be compromising/sacrificing for the
rest of our lives, at work, with people, and in all
our pursuits. Is the decision you're tasked with
something you can live and carry on with? No
matter what, you have options. We make mistakes
sometimes, maybe about that job, or new town, or
relationship. Just think things through as best as
you can and make peace with whatever you decide,
so that it doesn't hurt your heart the longer you
mentally immerse in the memories/worries.

Consider several perspectives in your deci-
sion-making process, since goals are ever-chan-
ging/evolving with our growth. And how one decision like moving to another country, and/or away
from family and friends could be both beneficial
and challenging. We don't get to see the future, but
we do get to decide how we choose to live our life
(stay in bed, watch tv, react defensively, assume,
attack, OR proceed/action). Continue working on
you, because we need to fight for ourselves.

Prayer is meditation. Prayer is believing and
connecting. Prayer builds on hope.
Talking to the Most Merciful, and obeying
His commands, through His Wisdom
can empower us to attain peace.

I gain insight into myself by unburdening the grip that pain has on me. Trusting Allah, the Most-Wise enables me to gain perspective of each setback/hardship. Recognising my thought pattern to then make decisions based on truth rather than imagined fiction means I'm making progress. I've found peace in my feelings, by asking for forgiveness and forgiving myself. I work on obeying the Eternal, the Illustrious. If we cannot ask for forgiveness, then we cannot, as a result, forgive ourselves. How does this affect our minds? How will the demon take advantage of this weakness?

Recognise your thought pattern and be the one to decide what makes sense going forward. What do you need to work on? What are your triggers? Use tools learnt on this journey of self-exploration to continue working through those issues to aspire for better days ahead. Who do we need to convince it is achievable?

Is your moral compass pointed in the right direction? Do you know the difference between right and wrong? Don't hurt another human being. Can it get simpler than that? But just as we must never hurt another soul, take a moment to think about whether or not you are hurting your own. Some may try unhelpful methods of coping which can lead them down a path they never thought they would adventure into.

ADDICTED

The scars of addiction just like the mind can take years to heal as we continue to work on re-directing. They may not necessarily disappear (the desire/want), but over time the intensity of this yearning will deteriorate. The fight is an inner struggle no person can understand but you. Allah, the Subtle One is with you and He understands you and your condition.

The seduction may pull you in, the escapism through pleasure will keep you coming back for more. You may find several hundred reasons to wrap yourself into a cocoon of nothingness. Feelings may become numb and the only driving force you may have is to return to a nonthreatening ordinary place.

Without a rock bottom or epic mistake, we could find ourselves in perpetual servitude of desire/escape.

Devoid of a reason to pull us out, we can physically remain within the land of the living, but mentally absent by chasing after anything that will soothe the emptiness that comes from enduring so much. What was your breaking point?

The scars of addiction may be as a result of something so devastatingly life-changing. We may redirect our thoughts, whereby the addiction takes over and we indulge in our pleasure senses by burying the pain. Lost in gratification by suppressing the anguish and inadvertently lose all control to feel, to taste, to perceive. A calculated act to smother all overwhelming senses/feelings.

In some shape or form, we are all pursuing pleasure. The pleasure factor can in some part be the healing or smothering of old wounds. The world is not an easy place to steer and emotions are too overwhelming to cope with at times. Whatever addiction you're faced with, the hurt in some cases will be strong and ever-present. Trying to numb the void from that demon seeking momentary pleasure brings us some comfort. Why else would we chase that which could also bring our downfall? At the time that it begins, it may be classified as one moment of weakness. We don't pay it much attention, because what harm could a little gratification bring?

We think we're invincible and perfect, able to stop at any time. Or in denial with a rationale that "It's not a big deal". The addiction becomes our push, our driving force and all productive plans and aspirations go out the window. As we're already dealing with so much, the pull of addiction is difficult to circumvent. Runaway from those feelings and we harm ourselves instead of exploring self-understanding, change, and growth.

Awareness, followed by want, followed by determination intertwined with action, are the stepping stones to recovery.

What are you addicted to and why? Have you explored what the attraction is and why this seemingly joyful release brings you back time and time again? The pursuit and act of hedonism will harden the heart (i.e. become impenetrable) to act/ feel or change for the better. Where has all the time gone? We can't learn the value of life in our significantly brief time if we do not experience loss, and some catastrophic incident to alter our point of view. Does our outlook stay the same throughout our lifetime or does it expand, advance, and re-shuffle? What inspires/motivates our change?

The fact is we do need to work, we need some form of structure and purpose. Work can be dull, challenging, and monotonous, threatening a hedonistic lifestyle. Without work, where does the purpose lie? Where does the desire to strive for more come into play? Where is Allah, the One Who Supports All in your life during this time? What conscious efforts do you make on a daily basis to try? To look beyond this life?

Hedonism is a sign of our level of attachment to this life, to people, to material things/even experiences. Happiness wears off its based on the momentary. Generally, it derives from the new e.g. new technology/new book/new clothes/new trip/ destination, new environment/new job/new baby/ new home, even food. What are you chasing? Aren't we all chasing eternal joy?

It is possible to keep a peaceful disposition alive through faith. Establishing gratefulness and contentment with regular vocalisation to Allah, the One Who is Free From All Blemishes, the All-Hearing. If Allah Azza Wa Jal is in our daily thoughts, and we habitually turn to Allah throughout the day (salaah), then shouldn't we be on the right path? When we have a true attachment to Allah, and controlled attachments to this life (i.e. within our grasp) we can be sure to keep fighting, and striving.

Hope indicates our attachment to Allah Subhanahu Wa Ta'ala, it demonstrates our reliance on Him, it shows we accept Him as being the One with Power, whereas we have none. A humbling act should weaken the ego, as the uninhibited nafs (self/ego) is a barrier to connecting with Allah. However, if we can connect, we can heal. We ought to think the best of Allah Azza Wa Jal because optimism can transform. The Power of Allah and His words (the Qur'an) knows no bounds. Miracles can happen! Change can happen! Don't let anyone tell you otherwise.

Since we redirect our thoughts to pull us into this tornado of emptiness (but still seeking pleasure), the answer to terminating this pull may also be to redirect our thoughts. By redirecting we can start a change in the pattern of behaviour no longer only seeking pleasure, and no longer burying the pain. Distracting tools can refocus our energies on other activities.

The addictive personality trait could be redirected to succeed and follow through with a belief that "This project will work." Because our belief in Allah keeps us going, Allah is the Light, the Illuminator. "There is no power except with Allah." (Surah Kahf 18:39). With redirection, we can find hope, purpose, and success again. They say life doesn't come with a manual to navigate through this confusing, mind-boggling, uncertain, unexpected terrain, but as Muslims, we have Allah's words (the Qur'an) and the Prophet's صَلَّى ٱللّٰهُ عَلَيْهِ وَسَلَّمَ example, and his sunnah. We need to explore what we reject or accept/obey, in order to gain peace, happiness, and fulfilment. It's a working progress of daily self-questioning.

So, when you decide for yourself that "It's time," know that your vision/plan/decisions will take a few hiccups along the way because you'll be finding your feet. Don't be disheartened, because the demon will want us to return to our old ways and abandon: our progress, a promising future, and beliefs. Giving up is just never an option when you decide on an ultimate goal i.e. the afterlife. As my mum and dad would say, "This life is nothing compared to what awaits us. But this life is all about sacrifices." In Sahih Muslim (2822) this message points out the struggle "Paradise is surrounded by hardships and the Hell-Fire is surrounded by temptations".

There are situations where we will need to change our approach or tactic. Until we face our problems head-on, we will always remain in this cycle of repeating mistakes by inaction.

THE INABILITY
TO ACT

Our inability to act is a strand of this critical disease. This mind, these thoughts, the anxiety, and this addiction can at times mean inaction. It is the combination of hopelessness, a lack of self-introspection, an abundance of self-criticism, and automatic self-assured doubt. In this arena, the demons within us become part of our everyday whole. There is little room for the possibility of there ever being more underneath this pessimistic paralysing cloud. Once the dissenting cynical demon attaches to us and we allow the gloom ridden thoughts of endless criticism to fester and overpower us, it becomes our identity. We often revisit past mistakes/arguments, and the people we either let go too soon or not soon enough.

We let ourselves wallow in the horror and disgust, that the immobilised remnants of Self are hardly recognisable. The inability to act may seem like the right approach at times when you spend time thinking over the situation. "This friend hasn't been there for me when I needed them. I'm feeling tired of being the one to put myself out there when I can't be afforded the same courtesy." Focusing on the disappointing feeling and not the times when this friend was available and helpful. Sure people change, and perhaps the friendship has fizzled as interests grow. Lack of time together also creates further distance.

The inability to act is connected to depression. It's too difficult to suddenly spring into action when we're told to, "Feel less," "Feel better," and "Let it go". These comments can be harmful to someone in an inactive state. The outsiders with no knowledge or understanding of this pain and struggle are tired of our methods of healing, or even regression.

We are all aware that being told to do something just because it's been asked of us, will not provide keen prolific results.

People are not wired in the same way. How can it then be said that an approach to dealing or moving forward will work in the same way for us all? Take a moment to think about all the people in your life; their different personalities. The subjects that compel them, the aspects of life they are passionate about, and the jobs/tasks they despise or enjoy. It's not fair to judge an individual's phase into inaction whatever the cause or reasoning behind it. However, it's worth reaching out to someone if you recognise it in them. Explore what it is THEY want, and how you can be of service to them. Working in harmony, not inharmoniously. Consider what they are going through, and only explore if they are amenable.

The world is not an easy place to navigate. People are tricky and complex. You think you have it sussed out but we all have irregular days and changeable moods. Truthfully aren't we all capable of a little something good and equally something bad. Sometimes it's directed at others and other times it's directed at ourselves. We hurt ourselves both intentionally and unintentionally. The frequent mistake is not questioning/exploring the reasons. Instead, desire is the prime focus without any provoking action or change. On the one hand, there's a push to avoid, and on the other, the push to succeed (similarly, a desire not to fail). Even with this knowledge, it can keep us within a stationary state.

We have moments of inaction because we need something more from our lives and more from someone that we aren't getting. We aren't seen or heard which brings us to a place to give no more than the minimum. Delay a text, or dodge a call for a few days. When it feels so overwhelming you may shut down and shut people out. Reflect-

ing on the Self in the most defeatist and obstruct-
ive way. Being consumed in self-pity instead of
communication and action. Repeating this perpetual cycle of nothingness, only becomes harder to
snap out of the deeper we dig. What reasons do
you give yourself when you decide to stop? What
reasons do you give before losing all faith/confi-
dence and trust?

Why is it that when experiencing failure we
lose hope, producing a fatalistic accepting nature
from just the one present mishap? The inability to
act may be due to the reminder of all past failures,
similarly reminders of all past hurt. The present
failure/hurt can't be seen as one entity but a string
of all that has gone wrong to create one colossal
whole. The reasons for why you are where you are.

Can the inability to act be altered and transi-
tioned into animation? Do you possess the power
to change your narrative? Have you been told by
someone or yourself that you can't? Or that it's not
possible? The inability to act is more than just the
words/reaction to circumstances and the people
who may partly be the cause of your metamor-
phosis.

Who/what do we blame for our inability to
act decades down the line? When do we decide to
energise? What tools support productive action?
What do you need to get there?

IMAGINATION

Imagination is a multi-faceted tool to encourage and build on hope. On the other hand, it could also be part of the denial, the denial of a disease, the denial of life and its troubles. We wish it away refusing to believe there is a problem at all. How many times have you said "I'm fine" but not truly meant it? Sure, it makes more sense to give a blanket statement than to delve into the complicated truth with loved ones at the family reunion, or with strangers, or even co-workers waiting in a queue for the microwave. Some will not mean you well or have any impact on changing (helping/alleviating) your current circumstances. In particular, we learn that sharing our truth may bring others a sinister joy to revel in our pain as a means to mock and denigrate.

My past Self would be drawn into a dystopian world, where I would conceal the pain and ignore (refuse to believe) any flicker of optimism. But just like addiction, I understood I needed to redirect.

*The imagination will either daydream/expect/
desire OR doubt/despair/discourage.
Which category do you fall into? Or a bit of both?*

In order for the imagination to have a positive effect on the now, it requires an examination
of the Self, our: needs, goals, and aspirations. All of
which require mental persistence/relentlessness.
A friend kept repeating, "It will happen," to which
I would always automatically respond, "But ..." "I
don't think ..." "It doesn't work out that way ..."
"That's not realistic". EACH and EVERY single time
she would reply, "It will!" Never losing hope, (never
frustrated with my scepticism), never giving up in
the certainty of our desires being fulfilled by Allah,
the Answerer of Du'as. I put a stop to the imagination, but she never did.

We put in the work, but Allah, the Praiseworthy makes success possible, through His Wisdom. You can have talent, but no 'luck' (chance/
miracle/surprise/unexpected opening), alternatively 'luck' but no talent. The 'luck' and talent I
attribute to the Invincible. The drive, the ability to
work (health), and resources (education/privilege,
even transportation and money for transportation) I attribute all as blessings bestowed by the
One Who Confessess Benefits. Nothing can work,
or move forward, or progress, or get better without
help or permission from the All-Powerful, the Ben-

evolent. Which is why you might have someone in your life insisting you renew (and work on) your connection with Allah Subhanahu Wa Ta'ala. Remember, a human being has limitations, we can't miraculously fix a problem overnight.

This imagination is like building an internal utopia fixated on internal and eternal peace. It is a form of healing which has had a ripple effect in my rampageous, overactive mind, as well as my relationships. I can walk away guilt-free, extricating myself before an argument can get out of hand. Being immediately cognizant of another person's disposition (irritability) can be empowering as it enlightens with the knowledge of:

1. When to stop, (stop talking, don't argue, don't stress your point of view, don't complain).
2. Walk away, (take a walk – because you feel your anger inflate. You are cognizant of your irritability as well as theirs. You don't want to distress anyone further).
3. Offer help by just listening/remaining calm, (know your limits, try to be helpful if you can).
4. Build a better understanding of the person (i.e. their triggers).

All of the above should formulate a healthier peaceful environment. How? Because we are alert to things: issues/situations/emotions beyond our own worlds (minds/struggles/day-to-day).

We possess the ability to break, shatter,
and tear others down.
Whilst also holding this immense influence
to reassure and inspire.

Contemplate the message you give out into the world, not just to the people in your close circle but beyond. What do you lean towards? Is it irrespective of who these people are, or what they have done/give you? Why should I try? If we cannot show mercy, it deprives us of Allah's mercy. And if I still can't... I need to question, what is this anger? Where does it stem from? How does the hate, jealousy, rage etc. in my heart affect my relationship with Allah Azza Wa Jal?

The faith/confidence in some people fascinated me because I wanted to understand, I wanted to dig deep and harness for myself. I was impressed by their behaviour and outlook, the control they exert over all they have accumulated and overcome in their lives. The tremendous discipline in dealing with malevolence, without being hardened by abhorrent, disparaging remarks. What have you learnt from the people in your life?

In this bubble of knowledge, I learnt how to get started. What is my part in constructing a neutral setting? I may not be able to open every single eye to behave with thoughtful regard and compassion for other people. However, I can at least spread some goodness that will long live even after I'm gone (I hope). What is your legacy? What do you think you'll leave behind? What impact have you achieved in a family, work/community/national/international level, or hope to reach someday?

I want to create a place with better mastery/command/skill/understanding of my feelings/thoughts/reactions. This is just a stepping stone. This imagination can serve a positive purpose by creating an inward strength to exude confidence, appreciation, and gratefulness in order to overcome troubles. Within our little world, we decide whether we want to stay, or move away and run. Do we use the fantasy to immerse into a realm of imagination to escape the inaction? The fantasy becomes the place we hold hope and find success; the idealistic world we long for. In times of great sorrow and debilitating change, this arena is a constant tool that holds me together. It necessitates healing through inventive imagery and inspiration. What is your imagination like? What ideas do you expand on? Do they encourage and motivate? Or do they wound and cripple?

I should point out that the creation of a fantasy world already existed in my mind. Brought on by the rise of anxiety. Which came first? I think they work together simultaneously somehow. This former fantasy served a purpose to panic, assume, and foresee possible/likelihood of danger and hardship. This fantasy-horror exacerbated my anxiety. It was an expedition to fright, yet I was drawn in because it was easily palatable and believable. I thought it was an asset (partly a safety feature), but I realise now it was detrimental as it suppresses hope. Scenarios and situations that never came to pass only extended my fear. Peace was an impossible concept.

I ask myself each moment I'm sucked into this harrowing vision of loss, grief, and trauma to STOP! Why am I losing hope without action? I'm a servant of the Most Merciful, why am I fearful when Allah Subhanahu Wa Ta'ala possesses all the answers and the power to change this situation. I have Allah, the Enricher, the Wealthy with me, so long as I turn with humbleness, belief, and **conviction**. Rerouting these explosive thoughts to succeed and inspire instead. I have to talk to myself, it's a way of unpacking those ideas and emotions.

Create a fantasy to escape. Not just so that you're in control, but once the world has been created in your mind we reach out for it. We draw into it further and further, building the coping tool, a vision. It could be the Jannah you aspire for, so the work in between (meaning now – this life) that we need to get better at, in order to get there. It's an exercise to boost optimism, for the things we want in this life too. Your vision and your aims.

For each person, we seek an escape from our misery focusing on what will bring us joy. Do not be confused with addiction, this is not a creation that will bleed you of sanity, introspection, and real-life animation (action). It's just a stepping stone to alleviate some of the everyday fullness of our minds. Whilst being aware of our attachments to these goals/plans. A healthy attachment (to work/succeed/gain etc.) will always remember the objective: Jannah. Nothing can trump this eternal happiness that awaits us. I pray Allah Azza Wa Jal gives us the understanding to grasp and maintain a balance of hope and fear.

Through the imagination, we CAN create hope (instead of fear), a step at a time. "There is no power and no strength except with Allah."

TRANSFORM-ATION TO REINVENT

There are a plethora of reasons for being drawn into the imagination, the main ones being the present is dangerous and pernicious. I am not fully in control, I am fragile and idle. If we seek what we desire uninhibited in fantasy, then why can't today be our new selves creating a new wholesome and healthy reality? There will be resistance and uncertainty, especially since fear and past mistakes often live too close to the surface of our minds holding us back. It will take some serious unquestionable gumption to construct this conscious very real life.

If you can reach the phase of imagination, (if you try, want to, believe in it, focus on it) then you'll be able to begin the process of instigation. Don't you want a revolutionised beginning contrary to the past? This willpower is capable of establishing hope by finding an internal purpose connected to Allah, the Kind Benefactor, the Ever-Pardoning. We can build a committed future, focused on being better in control and more forward-looking.

If we create a place of optimism within us, believe it to be true, then this strong foundation can unequivocally be created in the now too. Whether you call it manifesting, hard work, or exhibition, we begin by constructing it within us. Our connection with Allah Azza Wa Jal cannot be torn down by the temporary facets of this life. The Most Venerable is constant, and people are mortal, powerless, ever-changing, and unreliable. (Because we are not meant to be relying on them. They're on their own path striving for their own goals. Which is acceptable, don't begrudge them this, because we are too. But we don't do this selfishly, we can help others and help ourselves.) They are part of our journey (as we are a part of theirs), contributing to our lives in some shape or form, whether we get along or not. We accept and appreciate what they are willing to offer, without demanding more. Because demanding more leads to disappointment. Demanding more indicates our need (attachment) to them, rather than Allah Azza Wa Jal.

Believe in Allah, the One Who Suffices for Everyone and Everything, the Relenting, then act. Reach out for support/comfort/relief from Allah

Subhanahu Wa Ta'ala, the Supreme. Ask for help from a true friend/parent (a like-minded individual) and/or therapist who will assist and keep you on track. It's ok to stumble a little along the way as long as you preserve positivity with unwavering confidence in you. But most importantly, certainty in the One Who Gives All Things is with you if you work at it, and beg for it. What more do you need? Have you explored what is empty within you? What is operating and alert in our minds? And yes, sometimes things don't work out, but did you try, or did you give up? What are we pursuing and is it in line with what is considered an acceptable means of sustenance/work?

Faith is where hope lies, even when all seems like it is impossible.
Never forget that nothing, NOTHING is impossible for Allah Subhanahu Wa Ta'ala.

Self-criticism will hold you back. It may be ragingly vulgar as it has been tenaciously active for some time. It may cause you to doubt the One Who Causes Advancement, recalling past failures. The demon lives to torture us and in one way or another we let it in. We let the destructive villain in day after day, year after year, by obliging and conceding. As it's so ingrained and part of us, when an awakening spark of elation strikes it doesn't last. Since it's back, and back with a vengeful reminder of all we were never able to accomplish, and doubt we ever will. Horror scenes of past trauma and the pain attached to it can draw us into bad habits to lull the pain. Any prompt of the times you accomplished is consciously unhelpfully absent. This is your trial/affliction to overcome. And you WILL!

Did you create the demon and how? Was he created by a person closest to us, with their judgements, their hang-ups and their insensitive criticism? The parent who never believed in your talents, with a dismissive hand or a lack of support. Their nagging drumming of all the areas in need of attention under the pretext of 'teaching'. The egotistical sibling who bullied, mocked, and created a home competing for parents affection/time. How did the demon manifest and what power does he hold over you now?

Do you still pick apart how parents ally better with your sibling rather than you? Are you enveloped in your opinions when you spend time with your family because of hate or wounds you feel towards them? Maybe it's clear one sibling is the favourite, due to ideas surrounding the parent's ability to confide in one child but not the other. Or perhaps this favourite child has a way with the parent (manipulation) and it causes you heartache and feelings of unworthiness. If you are a parent, do you self-analyse? Do you act fairly?

How does it get better when we're dealing with problematic external factors? Care less, if that's possible? Walk away? Ignore? Forgive? To some degree, you have to let go of these emotional attachments and realise that your health comes first. Accept that you won't get from your parents/family the love/care/attention/thought or even apology that you want. Try to stop seeking it out, and create distance whilst maintaining the respect they deserve as parents/family and as servants of the Almighty. The more you question yourself (and how people make you feel, the approaches you tried and realised didn't work), the easier it will be to stop concerning yourself with those things in life which trigger heartache. Do the best you can.

Remember Allah, the All-Loving. Internalise and exude love.
It can calm the internal and will make the external more manageable.

A person is never just one thing, e.g. a daughter, a friend, a confidante/counsellor, a motivator, an athlete, a caregiver, a parent, a chef, a manager, a cleaner, a driver, an accountant, a doctor. We encompass many roles each day (and in a lifetime) which can be overwhelming at times.

Nevertheless, I see talent, skill, drive, and zeal in everyone. The varying degrees will differ for each of us, but we all possess the capability to try and overcome. And you have to believe that you can. You're transforming the imagination by embracing all these roles and more, it's an example of your tenacity and abilities.

I may not be able to animate confidence, or alacrity, or joyousness every single day but what is important, however, is the effort, the firmness/determination to keep trying. To look inwardly and unravel the reasons why I'm in a low mood. By lifting my awareness, I stimulate confidence in myself by recognising my plethora of skills and achievements. I am capable of bringing it all alive, with rules that I govern and decide upon. Ensuring that not even for a moment will I allow the demon in with hopelessness. Being mindful of not overextending myself, so that I can keep my sanity and my health intact. We need to check ourselves for whether we are ruled by our nafs/desires/ego or are we ruling it? Because without examining this (or keeping it in check) we could stray from the path.

Give as much as you can, but if you feel yourself being lost into a gloomy place, then take a step back and come back to self-reflection. Come back to the Self for healing. Return to the One Who Guides with the certainty of His power and His ability to vastly reform. Develop a balance of showing compassion to all around as well as yourself. Transforming the Self unlocks our potential. It means we can impart our encouragement, positivity, and helpfulness to others. As a result, improving our connection with Allah Ta'ala.

Don't give because you may receive, give because in the face of having to battle a cruel world we can be of help and comfort to others. Charity could be in so many forms (e.g. a smile, a gift, a ride, share a meal, giving someone a job/help to find work, money, support/listening, encouragement, sincere and helpful advice). And charity is the best thing we can do with our lives. All are likely to be experiencing heartache of their own (typically something you'd never expect). It could be post-partum depression, loss, suddenly widowed, miscarriage/s, divorce, difficult relationship/s, financial debt, physical pain, a worrying court case etc. The person sitting next to you on the bus may have just lost their child. Your doctor may have just found out they have a terminal illness. You boss may have spent the night searching for their parent with dementia, who decided to take a stroll. Your neighbour may have just had to put their pet down. Please remember to be patient, considerate, and lenient.

There are more people with blood on their hands than you'd think. And you and I may intentionally/unintentionally be pushing them to their limits. Transforming the Self, in reality, is a conscious awareness of needing to pause. Why? Because you may see a human being in pain by their actions, words, or demeanour/condition and this realisation ought to have you stop and be forbearing. However, for the most part, you won't even know when people are suffering, so be careful with your words – parents, children, family, strangers, and all. We'll never know the truth behind every smile.

To express kindness and to have restraint
is an example
of your awareness and understanding of pain.

What is restraint? Restraint means to hold back on our tongues, use wisdom in your interactions by refraining from short-tempered quick hurtful statements. Abandon a need to express every single complaint/opinion. Abandon the ego. How does ego/desire manifest? Do you think you're immune from it? Only if you're aware of it and have been working on it. What worldly desires do you hold dear? Test yourself by removing or limiting desire/compulsion for a day. For example, TV, phone (social media), other excessive habits, (e.g. food or sleep – can these be cut a little?) Can you fast randomly or be consistent on a chosen day?

We can transform by reminding ourselves how Generous and Kind Allah Subhanahu Wa

Ta'ala is. He has given us so many opportunities where our du'as will be accepted…

1. In salaah (in prostration/sujood) and after salaah. (That's FIVE times a day.)
2. Travelling.
3. Fasting.
4. In Ramadan. And Laylat-ul-Qadr (the Night of Decree).
5. Hajj and Umrah.

These are just a few examples. But if you have some time, look into others too so that you are making the most of these opportunities, and remember the etiquette of making du'a: praising Allah Subhanahu Wa Ta'ala (and recite His Magnificent Names in your du'a), reciting durood Shareef three times. Asking for forgiveness (look into this etiquette too).

When transforming to reinvent, remember you are the person in the driver's seat, giving in to the demon or rejecting the disapproving commentary. You hold all the keys, all the tools through lessons learnt in your life e.g. the mistakes, and the shortcomings. Even each misinterpreted screw up leading to an improved outlook picked up along the way. Just like children learning how to walk, stand up, fall, and get up again, we are more than capable of transforming and evolving. The effort lies within us, as we grow we can acquire this through self-reflection and self-love.

The fantasy could be as small or as immense as you desire and imagine. For example, speaking in a public setting, overcoming bullies, travelling, moving cities or countries. You hold the key, you are a force to be reckoned with, unwavering and loving. We can give to the world without diminishing our value.

In the beginning, the effort will need to be powerful, solidly concrete and impenetrable to combat the years of suffering. You might stumble, nevertheless divert your attention IMMEDIATELY from the seething internal force. Do not entertain and expand on the cynical thought, not for a second. Ask yourself, will you be the one to let the demon, the doubt, the anxiety, and the addiction in again? Are you consciously letting it in without an examination of the intent/cause or the repercussions? Are you ready to work on it?

What purpose are these contrary debilitating thoughts serving you, other than to perpetually torture and keep you from establishing a better life?

I can't despair! I won't! Even when my chest feels heavy with unstable wandering anxiety. I seek help from Allah, the Responsive One, the All-Powerful.

Create a better space of your choosing. Grasp it firmly and wholeheartedly in your mind. Transform it into your present. Unleash and unfold your beauty, your remarkability, and exceptional distinguishability. Together with the One Who Has The Power To Create Again, we can start fresh.

A DISCUSSION

Criticism is more important than positive thinking. Does that sound right to you? When did we decide that criticism was more valuable, more resolute? Do we strive to be better with criticism at the centre of our lives? Who are we competing with, and if comparing with others, ask yourself why? What is the purpose of comparing and who does it serve? Believe the criticism but don't trust the encouragement and supportiveness because it can't be altruistic?

The world can be a cruel place. There are more areas today where people spread venomous hate towards others. Often it's unprovoked and we have no control over how and when it approaches or from where. Good vs evil. Hate vs love. How tired are you of arguing with narrow-minded, ignorant people? Some are not willing to concede to their wrongdoings. In the heat of a moment, people will always stand their ground. Opposing voices exist in the world so how do we keep a middle ground to keep our sanity? I don't want to be the cause of someone's pain, as a result, I'll be quick to apologise and reflect to avoid a repeat of this mistake. Think about your approach, first to express your opinion. Secondly, how would you like someone to address an issue with you. By learning about the Self, we improve, elevate, and transform.

My value can only expand by leaving behind the toxically headstrong who add no value, but immense stress to my life. I recognise they may be dealing with pain of their own, so if I choose to speak up I do my best to make sure my words do not harm but are gentle. We transform by establishing an improved contented Self through movement in the present. It can be achieved when you feel ready in your own time. After working on detaching from the pain.

Pain can be a mortal or immortal beast depending on so many factors. It has the potential to survive in us (sometimes reliving it through triggers). The untreated build-up will make living impossible, as it tends to have a life of its own (for example, we may lash out, and feel easily overwhelmed). Do you recognise this? Do you have this in you now? Reflect on your suffering, and what you are holding in. It's not an intentional act to have this pain inside, after all, agonising bombshells (trauma, shock, injury etc.) in life take the wind out from us, like a loss for example. The pain will be intense at first and only time (where we process, self-reflect, question-self, try to heal, focus on the bigger picture, turn to Allah Azza Wa Jal) will help to alleviate this ache.

We will all have pain in us. And even with strong faith, we can still be shaken and be in pain. But it shouldn't turn us away from faith. We aren't robotic creatures, we feel. We can't easily cut off from our emotions, erase memories, remove/change parts we don't like, fast forward, rewind, or even sleep/turn off when we want to. When you're hit with something without warning its impossible to know how you'll react/feel/be/process or even understand the impact of this sudden development/circumstance/accident/incident. It will take time to regain your equilibrium. I know some will be harsh, unkind, and insensitive, but go easy on yourself. Isn't Allah Azza Wa Jal, Kind, Merciful, Most-Loving, All-Knowing?

So what's with all the pain then...? The process of pain is like a pilgrimage, to draw us closer to a purpose, to enlightenment. Enlightenment of what? Of the Self? Of a higher purpose? To experience something to make us more compassionate? To detach (to some degree) from this worldly life? Not to get caught in the illusion? To reconfigure our balance i.e. longing for the next life, not this life? The temptation of now (temporary) vs temptation of eternity (permanent)? To gain peace/comfort? It all comes down to changing us. You decide what pain is (and has been) to you. How has it impacted, shaped, and matured you? Eventually, the road leads to finding the Self and it ought to lead us to the Eternal if you're a believer.

Some will compare for us and expect us to be something they want, or believe to be better. Like our mental state, our path in life, or beliefs. It can put us in a defensive position having to explain why we've chosen a route. But we owe no one an explanation other than Allah, the Ever-Witnessing. What matters is what we put out into the world, what example we give, and how our limited time on this earth is used. After all, I am responsible and accountable for every action, every word, every harm in my own life. We mess up, but as long as we keep on asking Allah Azza Wa Jal for forgiveness (and forgiveness from those we hurt), and making an effort to change we shouldn't lose hope.

Human beings were not made to be perfect. We can stumble and graze our knees, BUT we can also pick up and carry on. What a huge blessing this is. A real example of the Mercy, and Kindness of Allah Subhanahu Wa Ta'ala upon us.

No person can truly understand your addiction, your conundrum, your difficulty, your agony. There are a few who will find pleasure in your suffering. Some will take what we say and either share it with others or find fault in our system of working through the grief to mock it. Others like to offer 'sage' advice. Like: get married, have children, pursue an alternative career path, because these suggestions and others will improve our lives. Really? Be careful when you think you know what is best for another person. Are you sure you know what they can bear? Are you aware of their relationship history, or their trauma, to understand what a suggestion like this could do? They have a life outside of your relationship with them, which means there are experiences you will not be aware of. Even a parent can't say they know their child 100%. We have no idea how children behave outside of the home (even their opinions, and the topics they discuss, and how they truly feel. Sometimes they'll be brave because they've been told to be brave. Or keep things in when they see their parents suffering, for example undergoing medical treatment, or dealing with loss). Ruminate over the ideas, experiences, or 'friends' you kept from your parents growing up.

Think about the advice/opinions you are offering. Would you say to someone whose been in an abusive relationship to, "Move on and find someone new"? NO! Would you ask someone, "When are you going to have children?" if they're struggling with infertility, or just lost a child/miscarried? NO! Suggestions are subjective, rarely taking into account the life of someone. We do not know what a person conceals, for reasons they only know.

We all need to recognise whether or not someone is in a position to hear what we have to offer. Don't approach it with an 'I know what you need' attitude or "It is my duty". If you say, "Get therapy" (for example) once, twice, thrice and we don't act on this advice then please grasp that this approach is not working. The worst thing an outsider (i.e. external to the pain/understanding/difficulty someone is experiencing) can do, is to nag and become impatient.

Similarly, when dealing with loss, people on the outside can sometimes be insensitive with their words. And for someone already in a mix of emotions trying to cope, and process/make sense of this sudden tragedy/jolt it can be hurtful to hear. Its like pain on top of pain. A broken heart is super super delicate, and maybe we learn what to express (or not and just listen) until we experience this type of pain first hand. A friend pointed out that, although people will say silly things, try to think of them as not deliberately trying to hurt you. It's also a reminder for me that I would have hurt someone too in my life (something I said that was silly too) so how could I not forgive. If you have a free minute (will take more than a few – but please please don't be deterred) type in a search engine 'sunnah to forgive' and have a read of what comes up. You should find Qur'an ayahs and many hadith. Why am I not listing them here...? Something happens to people when you say, "Its sunnah to forgive". Since every situation is unique I would rather in this case you look into it and internalise and grasp for yourself. I pray Allah Ta'ala gives us all guidance and understanding.

Some of the kindest things I've heard grieving the loss of my dad were people expressing their
memorable moments with him. Little things that
he did or said to them. So many things we had
no idea of until he passed. A neighbour said how
he used to help unload bags of groceries (whenever he spotted them) from their car to the front
door. Others said he would just say "Hello" and ask
how they were doing. People spoke about how he
always smiled. Later reflecting on this, I remem-
ber dad explaining that the Prophet صَلَّى ٱللّٰهُ عَلَيْهِ وَسَلَّمَ
was told by Angel Jibra'il (AS) to be good to your
neighbours (as well as parents, family, orphans,
and people in need). Even just a smile is an act of
charity. Dad would also remind us of this hadith
about Parents: The Messenger of Allah
صَلَّى ٱللّٰهُ عَلَيْهِ وَسَلَّمَ   said: "Every righteous child
who casts a look of mercy and affection upon his
parents shall be granted, for every look of his,
rewards equivalent to that of an accepted Hajj."
Those around the Prophet questioned: "O' Prophet
of Allah! Even if he were to look at them a hundred
times a day?"

 The Messenger of Allah صَلَّى ٱللّٰهُ عَلَيْهِ وَسَلَّمَ   replied:
"Indeed! Allah is the Greatest and Most Kind." (Bi-
harul Anwar, Volume 74, Page 73.) Dad made it a
point to tell us it didn't mean we didn't have to do
the official Hajj because of this reward. Hajj is com-
pulsory of course for those who can. When I remember this hadith it demonstrates Allah Ta'ala's

generosity and kindness.

Have faith at the foundation of your healing and progression. Regularly look inwardly to gauge how far you've come, and where you can improve. Recognise and accept the boundaries others set for themselves. Look at all the historical data you've accumulated about yourself, your experiences, and relationships. From your point of view, these facts give you a better understanding of where you want to be or don't want to be, and end up. As well as who you may choose to be with. Don't forget that we let the negativity in with the one thought, the one criticism, about that one crooked tooth, the unseasoned unappetising meal, the unamenable critical miserable in-laws.

*One negative thought will always attach
itself to another and another.
You'll have a story on your hands.
Real or fiction?*

Where did all the time go, after all, it was I who let those cynical thoughts in? While the thoughts festered and grew to become a formidable demon I could not expel without help, time (patience), and serious committed daily effort.

Our lives are more than the makeup of our little worlds where there has been unbearable worry and sporadic joy. Our lives are more than just a singular, it is made up of other lives and how we spread our energy because we are all connected. All that we leave behind (our legacy: positivity or negativity, reassurance or put-downs, inspire or discourage) will endure in the lives we touch in our short time here.

What do you embody and why? Because you are capable of overcoming, once you mind-fully keep choosing. Think about the Prophets in Islam. Their characteristics are an example/basis of what we ought to emulate. Most importantly the Prophet صَلَّى ٱللّٰهُ عَلَيْهِ وَسَلَّمَ . These aren't lesser people because they lived long ago. They relate to the now, if you're open to spending a little time studying, reflecting, and implementing.

If heaven is the reward, what more of a reason do you need to be elevated in this life and the next? There is this incredible blessing that we have of being in the Ummah of the Prophet صَلَّى ٱللّٰهُ عَلَيْهِ وَسَلَّمَ . But in order to recognise it, we need to reflect on this and why it is a bless-ing. On the Day of Judgement when we will all say, "Nafsi, nafsi," ("Myself, myself,") the Prophet صَلَّى ٱللّٰهُ عَلَيْهِ وَسَلَّمَ will say, "Ummati, Ummati." Truly, he was sent as a mercy to us. What does your heart feel when you hear this? Are you familiar with his (صَلَّى ٱللّٰهُ عَلَيْهِ وَسَلَّمَ) sacrifices, his selflessness? "Surely, there has come to you, from your midst, a Messenger who feels it very hard on him if you face a hardship, who is very anxious for your welfare, and for the believers, he is very kind, very merciful. But if they turn away, then say, (O Prophet), Allah is sufficient for me. There is no god (worthy of worship) except Him. In Him, I put my trust. And He is the Lord of the Mighty Throne." (Surah Taubah 9:128).

Keep examining the Self. Cling to exploring because tests will always be around the corner BUT with difficulty comes ease. Our outlook during the challenge/shock can break us, or give us courage and optimism if we "Hold firmly to the rope of Allah". Invoke Allah, the Oft-Returning by His Magnificent Names and seek forgiveness for your past shortcomings. Think about the sacrifices you can make to demonstrate an honest change going forward. For example, examine your point of view, behaviour, and attachments which take you away from Allah Subhanahu Wa Ta'ala. Your commitment to Allah will bring exceptional benefits, ease, comfort, and strength.

To humble ourselves in front of the Most Forbearing means to let go and accept the Almighty will intervene as He already does. Accept what is, and remember this message from the Prophet صَلَّى ٱللّٰهُ عَلَيْهِ وَسَلَّمَ :

"Wondrous is the affair of the believer for there is good for him in every matter and this is not the case with anyone except the believer. If he is happy, then he thanks Allah and thus there is good for him, and if he is harmed, then he shows patience and thus

there is good for him." (Sahih Muslim 2999).

I know what I have to choose to get better. What choices do you need to make? What ideas/conclusions have you made? Are you willing to explore all of yourself to overcome?

OVERCOMING OBSTACLES

Overcoming obstacles, struggles, weaknesses, challenges, and troubles are a few of the most agonising experiences in life that we must endure. The uncomfortable aspect of facing up to a mistake or disaster could leave you feeling like running out and away from it all. Oftentimes it may feel impossible to beat. This inescapable reality requires attention and strength to overcome. A gruelling but significant breakthrough.

By overcoming obstacles we identify our capabilities, tenacity, and endurance. Can you recall a hurdle you didn't think you'd ever get through? When recalling your past; the challenges faced, overcome and persevered, does it make you feel grateful its history? We are skilled at creating a defining moment when faced with obstacles, deciding upon a path that serves us well in the long run. Despite the fact it may be appealing to quit and make a run for it, the challenge was a means to enrich you as you built on strength and resolve. Do you think of it like this?

It is imperative to address an obstacle/setback/blow (when you can)
rather than fester in your mind where it can be blown out of proportion.

What would you say to someone trying to overcome an obstacle? Would you run down a list of things that have worked for you in the past or give them an example of a similar situation you faced? Think about the different approaches and examples you would give. Now think about what if it was you in their situation. Would it be helpful to hear experiences and advice on dealing with your specific problem? Some say yes, others no. We all want different things and what one finds supportive, another finds abhorrent, irrelevant, and condescending.

While it can be helpful to learn from other people's mistakes, their experiences are entirely subjective to them, (their personalities). This is through the lens of their childhood, and their upbringing. Influenced by parents, relationships, personalities, education, and experiences. What they need to learn and overcome, are challenges you may not have difficulty with, or ever experienced before. They may be the type of person who can be direct when a problem strikes. "You need to pull your weight. I can't keep covering for you, it's not fair on me." "That's racist." "What do you mean by that?" "That's not nice." For others, it may not be an area they're comfortable with. Speaking out may be something to work towards (within the boundaries of being polite/respectful, ensuring you don't hurt or act in a retaliatory manner). Act with vocal restraint to gain a better insight into the Self and others.

Oftentimes people can be a little too direct and thoughtless to the point of hurting another person. "That lipstick doesn't suit you." "Why can't you just eat everything like... at least she doesn't give me grief." "You're so greedy, I just bought this yesterday." "You need to change this style, so you'll make more money in your business." "I feel it is my duty to tell you..."

Be mindful of words that can be replayed,
producing wounds that may never/partly heal.
Sometimes silence is better.

Some people may never change. They may speak without any thought as to how their words will affect another human being. This may be as a result of their upbringing, pain/intolerance/irritability, and experiences. As a result, they see nothing wrong with using snappishly berating words. Similarly, they may just think they have something of value to offer, and think it might be helpful to the situation. These types of people may not be aware of the impact of their words on another soul. Perhaps no one has brought it up or had it pointed out to them. It's possible, they're just intentionally cruel, and we can never really know the reasons why.

When I refrain from speaking and watch this ornery person, I overlook the flaw and try to grasp the layers underneath the words. Are they in pain and reacting this way because they're overwhelmed or tired? They may have an aversion to me, in this case, I could leave. Or address this issue and figure out how we can construct a peaceful environment. When this internal grief is displayed externally it ought to touch my compassionate side (rather than react with annoyance or spiteful retort). If we immediately consider that this is a test from the Almighty, how could we proceed? How do we move forward? What is the best approach? I beg Allah, the Exalted to ease our suffering. I pray we can all improve our relationships (by starting inwardly) for His sake.

Do you have someone in your life who gives you unjustified distress? Is it demonstrated through an onslaught of harassment, explosive ranting, and relentless nitpicking? You may feel like you absolutely cannot pray for them, due to the pain they've caused you. It is a crushing state, I know. However, it is to test your capacity for mercy and compassion. Connection with Allah, the Lenient will help you to let go. Have you tried to pray for them, so that you can overcome and attain peace in the process? Peace can help us to overcome. And peace is attainable from the Giver of Peace.

When dealing with an obstacle and you need to talk it out, what approaches have you tried? Complain about the problem incessantly? Consider how life is unfair and this problem has reoccurred several times over? What if you could say to someone, "I'm struggling with something and I need you to tell me I can do this." "I need you to tell me I can get through this." Or, "I need help with a problem." What if you could decide what you need to hear without having to share the problem? Above all, without complaining, as this just brings the negativity back in. Would the solution or answer really change? Is it possible that you already have the answer? Reading this now think about the problem or roadblocks you're facing. How did they come to be present now, and why? What solutions will you explore? Are you energised, ready to galvanise? Or, will you stay where you are?

Are you a nurturer? Do you intrinsically care about others, putting others needs before your own? At times, we need to be selfless and other times self-regarding (all while demonstrating kindness, compassion, and patience). Recognise the difference between being caring to others, and ensuring self-care. Will helping someone today empower them, or refusing to help be a source of struggle? Will supporting someone disadvantage me in some way? Sometimes it's our pride, "I'm sick and tired of this. I'm helping this person but not getting anything out of this relationship." Supportiveness/assistance, showing kindness, and giving charity are all for the Most Merciful (yes, the physical activity will be for someone).

Establishing a type of detachment from good deeds means we empty our heart of human expectation (i.e. return, or even a 'thank you'). Only seeking the pleasure of Allah and His rewards.

Overcoming obstacles also means being aware that some people will take advantage of your generosity by constantly seeking you out. Giving in means they never learn for themselves as we silently (patiently) tell them this treatment is acceptable. Overcoming this kind of obstacle could mean setting boundaries, and ensure to stick within those parameters. If Saturday is the day you pick up groceries, stick with Saturdays. You can't do doctors' appointments but can arrange for another person to help out. You can't cook a meal every day, but meal prep instead to last a few days and show them (if they are able) how to prepare something easy (all depending on their capability). However, there are times we will need to be flexible too. Again, it comes to having the right kind of balance.

Take a moment to reflect on what you ask of people, and is it too much? What are they not expressing? How are they observing patience with you? We tend to forget the times a person was available/supportive/giving, instead, we focus on the times they weren't. Concentrating on the cynic, not the appreciative, means we need to inspect our heart and our own selves. Any motive which falls short of primarily being for the Creator is a loss for us in the long run. Do we have this forgetful attitude with Allah as well? Forget all that was ever given (every single morsel/drop of food/ drink – good news, happy moments, comfort, ease, shelter, leave and arrive home safely (you and your loved ones), or recovered from an illness) instead, emphasise what was taken away?

Getting stuck in a cycle of overextending yourself, may bring a cornucopia of ridiculous demands. Explain your situation, what you can/cannot do and remind yourself and them that fulfilling all their engulfing demands is unmanageable due to your work/time/energy/health. If you can see a solution like a sibling who isn't helping, a friend who could do a little, then point it out. Be clear but polite. Our options are: ask for help or suffer in silence. Never address the issue as a complaint as it will inhibit the likelihood of volunteered help. Laziness due to expectation sets in when you do too much. Allah Subhanahu Wa Ta'ala is the Giver of Strength, in time the situation will improve as you have accumulated extraordinary skills and wisdom dealing with complications.

These tests are not meant to break but prepare us, as we propel ahead with a better understanding of the world and its people. In turn, we strengthen our connection with our Maker. My main goal should be to please and obey the One Who is Free From Need, as I am always in need.

A sibling/family member may complain, refuse, ignore, and make excuses for why they can't help, but you worked on a solution and now you know to close this door. Sometimes until people are dealt with life the hard way, their hearts will remain impenetrable. Compassion and selflessness dead in them. The Controller of Hearts is All-Seeing, All-Hearing. I know it's tough. Well done for sticking through it for as long as you have. This anguish has not gone unseen. I pray the situation gets better and you find peace in your heart with the best solution. Keep making du'a, don't give up. Du'a is a means of incredible change, and release.

*We could regress into our old ways, never to
flourish by relapsing into former desires.
Or, mastering self-reflection and self-
questioning to continually evolve.*

Can you recall a time when you persevered?
For some, it's a little harder, because of the onslaught of challenges. It may have become a normal thought process when a challenge arises we
think about how life is crumbling. What happens
when we allow this harmful introspection to take
over? Do you contemplate scenarios in which you
avoid the problem; like move cities, change jobs, or
give up.

Regardless of whether there were times you
did give up you have without a doubt, even once
overcome a problem. For example, feeling anxious
about an interview/presentation but still tried it
out and gave it a shot. You may have stuttered,
or missed a point but you were present and active. You tried and the effort counts for so much.
Perhaps there was a time you were unsure about a
new job because you didn't meet all the skills cri-
teria, yet you still got the job. Did you stay, gave it
some time before you made a final judgement on
the job/staff and your capabilities? If the answer
was to move, change jobs, or give up, then perhaps

something better came as a result? Giving up repeatedly, time after time is a problem that needs to be addressed and overcome. And if you're willing, you may be able to find the answers within yourself by questioning and analysing. With a little time, trial and error you will find the right route for you.

The ability to conquer problems is in you, I do not doubt it. If this is what you seek then it can be achieved, whether you are consciously aware of it or not. The decision at the end of the day lies within you, to challenge yourself, and conquer. Or falter, never succeeding, never moving forward.

The possibility of more is limitless once you invite hope in, believing with determined optimism and unyielding expectation that more will come from Allah, the Source of Goodness.

Allah is the Giver of Sustenance and Strength, and He is a prayer away with incomparable, perfect knowledge of where the path will lead. This is the relationship where you give and give (sacrificing), never tiring. It will always be unexpectedly rewarded in ways that seemed impossible. But try not to turn to Allah, the Capable only in times of great sorrow and hardship. We always have to give, and if we are to see results we have to keep at it, through good days and the more challenging ones.

Never question why the prayers haven't been answered. It all just takes time. And remember, we do not have the foresight of what's to come. We do not know where the job/project or relationship will take us, but Allah Azza Wa Jal is always in full control. If you believe in Allah, and you are doing your best to fulfil your duties then...

"IT WILL COME. IT WILL HAPPEN. IT'S JUST A MATTER OF TIME."

"I am patient. I will not despair."

Don't give up hope. Don't give up asking. The tides can change as a result of your sincere, emotional prayer.

THE POSSIBILITIES ARE WAITING...

They lie in the Hands of our Creator

Reading this heading, what voice do you hear in your head? Pause for a minute and think this over. Are they imaginatively exciting (exploding), or convinced of the impossible? Allah Azza Wa Jal is the All-Powerful.

Nothing is impossible for Allah Subhanahu Wa Ta'ala.
"Glory is to Allah, and praise is to Him, by the multitude of His creation, by His pleasure, by the weight of His Throne, and by the extent of His words." (Sahih Muslim 4/2090).

We need to drum into our minds, that we

are worthy of forgiveness. We are not less than because we made some mistakes in our past that lead to addiction, or quitting, or other things. At that time we may have justified a need to exercise our desires to be free of the unbearable. But now... well, what do you want now? We need to remind ourselves of the love and forgiveness of Allah Subhanahu Wa Ta'ala, the Exceedingly Forgiving, and how living and breathing is a gift. It means we still have time to ask for forgiveness from the Clement, the Patient, and turn a new leaf. So don't wait till tomorrow, because tomorrow is promised to who? Allah is the Eternal, the Everlasting, not me, and not you.

We all make mistakes, but rotating/recapping these memories (i.e. the mistakes, the negativity, the hopelessness) can weaken us. By allowing the demon in with harsh unencumbered negativity, we cannot shine. He wants us to despair so that we do not turn to Allah, and reject our faith instead. But to heal, to have peace/Afiyah (wellbeing), and to move forward we need Allah Azza Wa Jal. Only Allah, the Most Gentle can truly give us what we seek. We can maintain and strengthen this bond through salaah, which is the most fundamental part of faith. The comfort salaah can bring to our hearts lies in the commitment of this **frequent** act of **attentive** worship.

I think it's special that all we have to do is call out to Allah Subhanahu Wa Ta'ala, the All-Aware and He listens. There is no phone call, waiting on hold, or waiting in a queue. He doesn't ask for a payment, and we aren't limited in the time we have Allah, as we do with people/therapists. He never tires of us. He loves to hear us call on Him. He has all the answers. If we are willing to iron out time for Allah Ta'ala (e.g. our obligations), you have truly grasped the strongest handhold there could ever be. If you have Allah Azza Wa Jal, you have everything. "Whoever disbelieves in Taghut (e.g. false gods, idols, devils, and seducers) and believes in Allah, then he has grasped the most trustworthy handhold that will never break. And Allah is All-Hearer, All-Knower." (Surah Baqarah 2:256).

The possibilities are infinite is a hopeful place of wonder to get to, to aspire to, to apply all our efforts and energy. Even just contemplating this 'magic' fills my soul with unshackled energy. It's taken some time to get to this anticipative place of dreaming and ambition (within boundaries of Islam), in addition to the difficulty of maintaining the unshakeable joy that arises with achieving. Why? Why is it important? Because pain dominated my world and I was exhausted with an 'I'm done' attitude. There was no care of the Self, including no desire for a future. What is in your heart? What do you feel? What mental state do you want to get to achieve/maintain?

"Ya Allah, the Perfect, the Most Great, the Invincible,

the Self-Glorious, please grant us all exceptional, extraordinary, magnificent, multiplying, unlimited, unexpected: barakah, bounties, and blessings in this life and the next. Open our eyes with gratitude to the bounties you have already, and always given. Help us to look to the future with hope and trust in Your perfect planning, kindness, and care towards us."

There is a larger purpose in all our lives, which must include Allah, the Everlasting. Keeping the faith means we must work on expanding our knowledge to action/reform and implement. If you are a believer then you know this is your supreme goal and purpose: to please, obey, and worship Allah Azza Wa Jal. How much time do you spend contemplating the afterlife? What type of afterlife do you envisage for yourself, taking into account your past and present actions/behaviour/attitude? No one can truly know (even when they try to guess or judge) the sincerity of your heart (concerning faith) except for the All-knowing. No one knows how much you pray, or do for Allah behind closed doors (and in your mind, like dhikr, du'a, sadaqah etc), except for the Supreme. Only Allah Ta'ala can judge our righteousness.

The transformation of the fantasy will mean working on the Self now to obtain it so that it can become reality in the next life. We cannot bank on a little good deed here and there to be enough to reach Jannah. We can't know until the next life, which acts were pleasing to Allah. We are meant to be in a state of unceasingly improving our character. We can expand our desires and amplify our purpose through the exploration of possibility for this life and the next. As a result, developing inner fortitude and drive, by understanding the Self. It doesn't mean to be obsessed with the achievement of this life, it's just a stepping stone to grasp hope and imagination. To feel again. To want again. To care again. To try.

When I was little, my parents would have us (my siblings and I) talk about all the things we wanted in our Jannah. There was no limitation except for our imagination. You might be able to guess (from a child's perspective/idea/desires) that it meant we asked for a lot of chocolate and sweets. It was an elated spark, inciting so much hope, and love for Allah Subhanahu Wa Ta'ala. We never doubted that it wouldn't become a reality. I visualised (begged/asked) for trees of chocolate bars, and fruits. Each time I would take one, another would miraculously emerge in its place. Unusual methods of retrieving drinks/soda, my own ice cream and milkshake machines with all the flavours I could think of. My own bakery with buttery pastries, hot bread, and fruity jams that I could help myself to whenever I wanted. I also wanted a theme park (no queues!), a doughnut shop, a drive-through burger place, a farm/ranch with all sorts of animals; especially giraffes and horses. Also being able to fly and travel. Have you ever wondered what it would be like to swim in sprinkles? How about space travel? (I know, my imagination was/is a little... funny...?) Even amidst all the delight, I think the best part would have to be: no more physical, internal, and external pain, AND no more toothaches! (Which may come as no surprise considering my enjoyment of sweet treats.)

As you can tell, the ideas were wild with joyful exhilaration – although, mostly related to food, I know! Was there anything you dreamt of as a child? Is there anything you dream of now? Does it make you smile, fill your heart with hope and excitement? I pray we all reach Jannah and find that Allah Subhanahu Wa Ta'ala from His Mercy, Generosity, Perfection, Kindness, and Love, will gift us with all the things we once dreamt of. Plus all the things we didn't think to ask for because it seemed too silly, or too impossible. Remembering these moments of daydreaming helps to invite happiness in. It's a place of possibilities to get back to again for this life and the next. It's an encouraging, hopeful reminder of a paradise that awaits us (on the condition that we are willing to work for it of course).

As children, we understood that doing good meant getting something good, or even remarkably spectacular in the next life. But we grew up, and life became... so we gave up a little here and a little there. And accepted that doing anything, achieving anything was HARD WORK! (When we remark/decide in our minds that something is hard work, it will be. The challenges are all we will see, and we will not be able to see anything else.) We also clasped disappointment and became enlightened through loss and heartache. Recalling the past could be both elatedly cheerful (like planning my heaven, remembering my dad) as well as heartbreaking (remembering my dad, his last moments, and still getting used to him not being around. Also fixating on the harsh burden of just existing – because my outlook was such).

Pain or joy is in all of us and we are capable of living with both. But when you get to this place of possibility, it can become transformative! How? HOPE which develops into STRENGTH! It's the redirection and twisting of thoughts – like searching for the silver lining which somehow removes a little of the outer shell of discomfort that takes a point of attaching to the heart. (I pray we are reunited with our loved ones, and for me this is a comfort. This is my silver lining. May Allah Ta'ala grant us all hidayat/guidance.) Detachment. Detaching for me in this context meant remembering the good memories otherwise all else is too soul-crushing.

The One Who Exercises Responsibility Over All Things can open the doors of possibility, of opportunity, of healing for us. In the same way,

Allah, the All-Perfect can help us to heal and close the doors of an overwhelming past for us.

I have been desperately (after each salaah, and during the day when I remember – it would be more appropriate to say – when Allah Subhanahu Wa Ta'ala reminds me – "Praise be to Allah") holding onto this ayah from Surah Talaq: "… And whoever fears Allah - He will make for him a way out. And will provide for him from where he does not expect. And whoever relies upon Allah - then He is sufficient for him. Indeed, Allah will accomplish His purpose. Allah has already set for everything a (decreed) extent." (65:2-3). Take a moment to grasp what this means. There are some incredible talks, and remarkable stories online attached to this ayah. I hope you look into it for yourself. The words (i.e. the ayah, but remember these are Allah's words) gave me hope (Allah Ta'ala gave me hope) and a prompt of the conviction and concentration (and passion) I needed to have in my du'as. "IT WILL!" Just like my friend would assert.

I'm doing my best to just keep moving forward with Glorious help from our Creator, the Most Loving, the Sustainer of Life, the One with Veneration. My heart fills with anticipation, and a stronger sense of connection with Allah. This ayah (as well as others) was one of many it 'clicked' moments. Something filled the void as I enforced (reminded/repeated – in Arabic) these amazing words of Allah Azza Wa Jal, the One Who is Free From All Distress, the Clement. Do you have an ayah/s which speaks to you?

Work on a purpose and move forward with intention. Anything we start in life always feels impossible at the outset because we're looking at where we need to get to (i.e. the end) and all the work needed to be done in the middle. For example, memorising the Qur'an. You'll start on page one with hundreds of pages to go. It can be intimidating if you concentrate on the big picture. But break it down into pieces/stages. One surah at a time (or line at a time). Next thing you know you've learnt one surah, then ten, then twenty, then one suparah/juz. And why would we make this effort? We have a choice of either sticking with the ten surahs we learnt before the age of 10 and insist we have no time now to learn, or we're too old, or it's too hard. Or showing Allah Azza Wa Jal that we are sincere and honest about self-improvement, and seeking forgiveness. Do you think about meeting your Lord? I pray Allah Ta'ala returns us to Him when He is pleased with us.

Our goals/hopes may seem unmanageable, but you can get to this place of possibilities, and you WILL. At some point even the goal, won't feel like the finish line, there may be some bumps/ roadblocks along the way and your direction may need to be diverted or re-routed. The truth is there isn't a finish line (in the worldly sense), where we are blissfully content because other aspirations will follow with new needs and hurdles that arise. Followed by innovative ideas, new people, and unpredictable adventures too. All of the above continually open our minds to more. And when more means connecting to Allah, connecting to the Prophet صَلَّى ٱللَّهُ عَلَيْهِ وَسَلَّمَ , working on ourself (internally and externally), and spreading good, then more (in this regard) will always be fulfilling/satisfying.

We evolve, we change.
We tackle a challenge, after another, and another.

We are creatures seeking fulfilment, and we cannot cease working or it unsettles our soul and mind. It can lead to despair, doubt, and hopelessness = unhealthy contemplation. I ask Allah, the All-Perfect, the All and Ever-Witnessing, the Absolute Truth, for ease, for relief, and answers.

The possibilities are beyond limits: if I can construct a case to get up in the morning, pray, make the bed, have a shower, and clean up. If I can force myself to make breakfast. If I can boost optimism. If I can give all that I can in relationships without feeling burnt out. If I can focus on one thing, or one objective and gradually work from there. Time, in addition to healing (e.g. prayer, introspection, self-analysis, implementation) and distance (e.g. time out from work, and away from people/unnecessary discourse), has allowed me to work on altering my mindset to a place of opportunity. But the best part is the peace due to the above actions/habits, in addition to expressing gratefulness throughout the day, in speech and in prostration. It is undeniably imperative to consciously disengage from the internal negativity (thoughts) and external pessimism (discourse). Peace is attainable by continually learning about our deen. Peace is attainable from Allah, the Giver of Peace.

"Ya Allah, O the Flawless, Remover of Fear, Giver of Tranquillity, bestow us with: internal, external, and eternal, Afiyah, peace, and satisfaction."

Believing the possibilities are multiplying by Allah, the Giver of All Things, the Most Generous, the Disposer of Affairs empowers me to crush the demon as I decide on a path ahead. It empowers me because I know Allah Azza Wa Jal will bring me good as I actively explore the bright side in every single situation. He is in full control. I can work through the problem, finding a solution appropriately tailored to my needs. I can do Istikhara – ask for guidance when I'm unsure what path to take. (Have you ever read/contemplated the meaning of the Istikhara du'a?) The mentality can change from spinning negatively, with suspicion and doubt in ourselves and others, to accurate assessments (communication and confronting a problem), and talking to Allah, the Watchful, the All-Hearing.

I can either dive into ideas of "I wish," when I think of my dad, or I can use the time I have now until my last, to carry on working so that he can gain rewards too. The kindness we exhibit towards our parents doesn't just end when they leave this world. There is so much we can do for them. Sadly the loss is irreplaceable (as you would expect) but with this ache, I do my best to redirect in the form of deeds that can (Allah willing) benefit him and others. I pray Allah forgives and preserves our parents, keeping them well and healthy. And help us to improve our relationships, so that we can make the most of the time we have with each other before its too late. The Prophet صَلَّى ٱللّٰهُ عَلَيْهِ وَسَلَّم said: "A man will be raised in status in Paradise and will say: 'Where did this come from?' And it will be said: 'From your son's praying for forgiveness for you.'" (Sunan Ibn Majah 3660.)

If a wave of unfounded worry takes over, it's a signal to pause. It's an indication to rewrite the internal monologue, to stop the insatiable

bleakness from snowballing mistakenly.
Ask yourself: What are these thoughts? How
do they impede growth/accomplishing?

Negativity destroys inspiration! A conviction and emphasis on the capability and abilities of the All-Powerful, the All-Strong, can eradicate all dissenting thoughts. It's a matter of focusing all my confident energy and strength, into an idea that will undoubtedly come to fruition. A firm optimistic attitude keeps me functioning through constant drumming and reminder; "I have to do this." "I have to make it work." "Don't think about the scepticism in others, this is my journey."

The possibilities are expanding if I can spend time in the service of others and humanity. I can create positivity by building others up. I can be the light in their time of need. Just as some have been there for me. I can be the non-judgemental confidante, motivator, mediator, personal grocery shopper, hospital appointment companion, housekeeper, or chef. The mammoth firework display is of aspiration, beauty, and awe.

All the possibilities, all the encouragement, and good that I put out into the world starts by first believing in it. One empty day is contagious. One empty day is fatal to my mental health. There are many layers to an empty day but there is good in each day if I can unravel it as such. Even if I've spent the day at home with basic needs met (like five daily prayers), it's a day of rest to rejuvenate, to recharge.

As I open my eyes, I'm grateful for my home, for shelter, for warmth, for a bed and blankets, for running water, for electricity, for my electrical products. I've slept, that's gratitude. Or had insomnia, that's gratitude too because I could make du'a in the middle of the night (so long as I resist the urge to check my phone unnecessarily). I've prayed, that's gratitude. Eaten, that's gratitude (with more food in the cupboards, is gratitude. No problem eating – A BLESSING). Taken the time in the morning to breathe in and revel in my cup of coffee, gratitude. Warm water to shower/do wudhu, that's gratitude. Clean clothes (a working washing machine/dryer/sunny weather), that's gratitude. Seeing the sun, growing my plants, that's gratitude. I'm obsessed (in a non-harmful way, I think?!) with basil – it makes me happy. Smells gorgeous, and is superbly scrumptious! Glory be to Allah. Seeing the rain, feeding my plants (water for us too of course), that's gratitude. Seeing family and friends smile, healthy, fed, and return home safely is gratitude too. All and more is thankfulness to the Creator, praise be to Allah, the Obvious. How often do you vocalise it? What topics/aspects in your life do you convey your appreciation for, or do you withhold gratitude?

With gratefulness, the All-Giving has promised to give us more. The lens of optimism can either be easy or hard to find, depending on you. Gratefulness will please the Almighty. Complaining, however, will only bring further worry with a fruitless end. Allah, the Knower of Innermost Secrets awaits our sincere humble call. Are you familiar with this ayah in Surah Ar-Ra'd 13:28: "Those who believe and whose hearts find rest in the remembrance of Allah. Verily, in the remembrance of Allah do hearts find rest." Why do we find rest with the remembrance of Allah Subhanahu Wa Ta'ala? Our soul, our being, is incomplete, unsettled, broken, and in pain without Him. Have you ever closed your eyes and tried to meditate/calm yourself/connect by repeating "Ya, Allah. Ya, Allah. Ya, Allah."

The possibilities are boundless because I won't accept defeat. When failure and challenges come my way, I will be determined to carry on a path onward. It may be an alternate path, but I can accept not to make it a rigid one. This flexibility keeps me whole and together. I just have to figure out how at that moment (a fragile moment, with fear, anxiety, sadness, overwhelming emotion) I can take charge to alleviate my distress. And of course, we have to take our time to process and deal with our emotions. There is no quick fix.

To avoid is to give the demon longevity, but
to tackle this issue attracts hope.

*Action gives us vitality. We fight for
our lives, for our afterlife.*

The possibilities are evolving because I have the answers I need. I won't regress. I can reflect on the past without having it perpetually destroy and cripple me. I will **adapt** to the path ahead. I am stronger than I was yesterday as my re-trained automatic response will evoke confidence, thinking the best of Allah Subhanahu Wa Ta'ala in every situation. My set of coping tools will keep me steadfast, self-assured, and tenacious. Rest is essential! Prayer is indispensable!

The doors of possibility are opening. Faith is a gift, a blessing, it is our armour. Allah Subhanahu Wa Ta'ala gives us strength. Allah is our Protector.

IMPLEMENTING THE POSSIBLE

Implementing is an indication of progress. So how does it look in practice... you fight the internal telling you to lie in, not to pray, not to go for a walk, not to take a phone call, not to help someone. Fight the internal telling you to yell, to fight every single disagreement, to voice an opinion, to justify inflicting pain. Fight the internal preventing you from changing by not questioning the Self. What happens when you listen to this voice? And what happens when you don't?

Implementing can start small like buying a sandwich/snack/drink for a homeless person or handing over some loose change/cash. It could also mean a shift in how you interact with people. How does this adjustment affect learning about the Self, and the expectations on us as Muslims (to be patient, to give our time etc)? What do you want to start implementing? What is the absolute non-negotiable thought/action you want to put into effect and why? Is it centred on faith and the bigger picture (i.e. the eternal next – meeting Allah Subhanahu Wa Ta'ala), or only engrossed/obsessed in this worldly life?

Implementing could be starting each new activity with: "In the name of the Most Compassionate, the Most Merciful," (بسم الله الرحمن الرحيم). Like getting up, getting dressed, walking out of the house, stepping onto the train/bus or getting into your car, eating, (there are also du'as for these activities – and more, which you may already know.) Nurture the remembrance and awareness of Allah Ta'ala. A healthy start in remembering Who we belong to, and Who we will return to.

Implementing could mean taking your shoes and clothes off with the left side first and putting them on with the right first. Being mindful of whether or not you leave the water running when you do wudhu, or conserve water by using just enough. You could increase recitation of Durood Shareef upon the Prophet صَلَّى ٱللَّٰهُ عَلَيْهِ وَسَلَّمَ to obtain barakah (blessings) and forgiveness. Amongst other benefits, like ease to your difficulties/troubles. I ask myself regularly, have I prayed enough Durood Shareef for the Prophet صَلَّى ٱللَّٰهُ عَلَيْهِ وَسَلَّمَ ? And if not (which I feel like is never enough) iron out time to make sure you do (and if you're forgetful, like me, sincerely ask Allah to help you to remember). If we are immersed in an activity (watching TV, listening to music, gossiping, or engaged in some outdoor activities – think about what these activities could be) in which we wouldn't be able to recite Durood Shareef, then this activity is taking me away from Allah, and His Mercy, and possibly giving the demon access through these mediums. We all need Allah Azza Wa Jal's Mercy, now and forever.

Implementing may start with one lecture/bayaan/halaqa (a day/week, even a video online). Passive learning without note-taking may not have as big of an impact as one we take notes in to revisit (it becomes a proper lesson in this form, as you demonstrate your keenness to learn). Otherwise, we just consume and consume like it's entertainment without reflecting on how we apply these reminders (mentioned in the talk) to our lives. First and foremost, do work on your five daily prayers, this is critical for relief that only Allah Subhanahu Wa Ta'ala can give. We are all responsible for this so just try.

Implementing from within (is just as important as the external habits) could be: noticing how you react with certain subjects or with certain people. The kind of person you do not want to be in these scenarios. It could be that you react poorly with a family member due to a painful past, so you either avoid them, the subject you argue about, or limit your contact, whilst understanding the need to obey Allah Azza Wa Jal.

In addition, you could implement new practices, like going to bed early without your phone so that you are not tempted to read the news before sleep. Being aware of the effect of problematic external factors on the internal will help to maintain peace. Persistently expand on aspirations to create an internal promise to keep pushing no matter how herculean.

The right kind of help differs for each person. Simply ask Allah, the Eternal and watch how extraordinarily the pieces will fall into place even if it's the courage to get help. The possibilities are unlimited because you have Allah, the Deviser on your side. Be patient, keep trying/working, and persevere, for the One Who Confesses Benefits is with you.

Be consistent with your pursuit: to live a healthy, grateful, contented life.
Be consistent with your development: learning, reflecting, nurturing, praying, implementing. Our existence is more than just work, more than the difficult relationships, and more than our thoughtless limitless worldly hunts. What do you want deep down?

You are valuable because your story has been built with a bigger picture in mind. We just don't possess the wisdom to comprehend it. Someday it may click (in this life or the next)! Hold onto Allah Subhanahu Wa Ta'ala. Hold onto miraculous optimism. Hold onto phenomenal possibilities. Hold onto your vision. Or the 'magic' (excitement) you feel when you contemplate opportunity e.g.

Jannah, Hajj/Umrah, a project, work, education, job, business, travel. This excitement is no small feat considering what you have overcome to get here. Entertaining the thought is just a catalyst for more. You ARE capable of getting to this place, and what an achievement when you do. (Always have the upper hand when it comes to self-awareness, examining your attachment to the new.)

> *Contemplate how your experiences*
> *have been an asset to:*
> *educate, enlighten, and empower.*

Use that internal barometer to recognise the danger in dissenting thoughts and assumptions when approaching a difficult situation or person. Look for clues on your/their mental state to be able to support, not harm. Reflect on those life experiences, fortunate and unfortunate circumstances because you bring something worthwhile to the table, with your exclusive collection of wisdom and insights.

If you've made it to this point of my perspective (my critique, my erratically alert mind) then I know you've lived. I know you've faced struggle and challenges. And just as you have gotten through those difficult times, you will also get through the present too, and the future struggles to come. Allah Azza Wa Jal is the Answerer of Du'as as long as we keep the Restorer, the Reinstater as our primary focus every single day.

I can't promise there won't be challenging times ahead. But I can promise that even amidst bleak uncertainty, hopeful confidence will follow. Say goodbye to that part of yourself that has historically never dealt well with hardship and heartache. Only making it worse by overthinking, by trying to please others, by taking on too much. One attempt at a time is all we can manage sometimes. Leave the injurious internal narrative in the past.

"I am more a fighter today than I was yesterday, just as I will thrive and persist to be healthy for years to come."

FAITH

Faith is a sensitive topic, which is why I've kept this section for the end. Are you aware of this? (Although, dispersed throughout this book as I believe faith is key to healing and opening the eyes to our broader purpose. Shifting our thoughts so that we can self-reflect and improve.) Why do you think faith is a delicate subject? Is it the approach of the people in our lives? Their rigidity? Lack of understanding? The overwhelming fear of Hell and the Day of Judgement? Our sins? Repercussions? Accountability? Fear in general?

You need a bit of wisdom to know when the right time to bring up certain subjects would be. Faith can be a difficult one, due to the relationship we have with a forcing person (like a parent for example), also their approach, overwhelming lack of understanding/empathy, and rousing fear. What approach brings people in and what approach turns people away? Nurturing can be lacking do to others own fears/hang-ups/ideas/interpretation.

It is so vital that we are mindful about what

we say to someone about faith during an anxiety attack, or suffering with depression, or other mental illness. They don't need harsh abrupt words; "You have to pray." "You'll go to hell if you don't pray five times a day." They need a gentle touch: "You want to talk?" "Want some help?" "I don't know how to help, but if you want we can pray together." "I'll make dua for you, it will be ok." Either this or just leave it alone altogether, because in these situations the suffering will react out of character and lash out. And anything they say at that moment can never be erased.

You may be familiar with what works and what doesn't. If anything, concentrate on the attributes of the Most Merciful: the Invincible, the Remover Of All Difficulties, the Powerful, the Caretaker etc. and educate yourself. Your actions/ words/demeanour can invite people in or turn them away. Set a better example. They'll come around in their own time, Allah willing. Make du'a for them in the meantime. The state of their mental health matters because they will be receptive to you. They will either ruminate over your kind and patient words or shut down and throw in the towel. And you do not want this. There is only so much we can do to alleviate the suffering of another person. Which is why parents suggest turning to the Most Loving, because He won't disappoint, and He CAN HEAL ALL WOUNDS. It shows the extent of help a human being can give to someone in pain. Getting better always comes down to the individual putting in the work themselves.

At the end of the day, we all know we need to pray five times a day. As far as I know, there are only a few exceptions. So we know at some point we need to kick it into gear and get started. There are several reasons which prevent this humbling, begging, expecting, and waiting. If you're an outsider of mental health, and you are trying to help someone, you may be thinking, "What am I supposed to do?" The best thing is to pray for their hidayat and yours too (because we are all a work-in-progress). Don't give up. Don't get frustrated because they don't listen and you don't understand when prayer makes so much sense to you. They need you and your du'as. They need help, but an intervention in which they are open to it. Was there a time in your life where you didn't pray? What was the reason you didn't? Prayer (submission to the Creator) is an integral part to attaining peace (but work has to go into it, and you have to want to do it in order to feel it). In time (because the shift happens one day when we don't think to expect it), I pray we all get there.

We have all had that moment (or several) in our lives which were so intense you didn't know if you were going to make it. These trials need attention because they caused a type of damage that changed us and sometimes in a negative way. You may have become short-tempered, a cynic, a recluse, avoiding a certain type of people or activity due to the trauma. It is essential to healing to let it out, talking and tackling the issue once you're ready. The get-up and ready attitude must emanate from you. Keep in mind the type of people you talk to, and how experienced they are in addressing your problem if this is the route you choose to take. Most importantly, you will always have the One with an Exalted Position each moment of each day. Without communication, we cannot get to the route of distress. It just shows that we need support. We need to educate ourselves, we need to know how to improve areas of our life which can come with therapy/self-analysis, and reflection. Then we'll be ready to execute and perform.

"Ya Allah, O the Glorious, please ease the uneasiness in our hearts, remove the distress, the heartache in our lives. Help us to understand, mature, overcome, and move on."

No matter the issue, whether it's in the internal or the external I always come back to introspection, critical thinking, and most importantly Allah, the All and Oft-Forgiving, Giver of Gifts. Faith is a stepping stone to healing, so doing your best will mean to keep learning, and implement what you can. As much as you can manage at a time.

Learning about the life of the Prophet

صَلَّى ٱللّٰهُ عَلَيِهِ وَسَلَّمَ and his sunnah is significant (and essential) to better connect with him صَلَّى ٱللّٰهُ عَلَيِهِ وَسَلَّمَ. Why? I remind myself of his sacrifices, he deserves a great deal of respect. The pain and suffering he endured should pinch at my heart so that it compels me to follow his example. So ask yourself, do you love the Prophet صَلَّى ٱللّٰهُ عَلَيِهِ وَسَلَّمَ? How do you show this in your day-to-day? What do you implement/teach/share/give/demonstrate? Do you love him more than you love yourself? Do you wish to meet him, dream of him, emulate him (صَلَّى ٱللّٰهُ عَلَيِهِ وَسَلَّمَ)? "None of you have faith until I am more beloved to him than his children, his father, and all of the people." (Bukhari 15, Muslim 44). If we can love the Prophet صَلَّى ٱللّٰهُ عَلَيِهِ وَسَلَّمَ more than our own selves, it means we've overcome our nafs/desires. Because to follow means to believe wholeheartedly, which means to be on the right track. I pray we all get to meet him (صَلَّى ٱللّٰهُ عَلَيِهِ وَسَلَّمَ) one day and drink from Hawd Al-Kauthar.

I heard a story where someone had a dream of the Prophet صَلَّى ٱللّٰهُ عَلَيِهِ وَسَلَّمَ. He was saddened that the Ummah were not fulfilling/following his sunnah. That we had left him. It made me think, how much do I actually do?

Now you could take this story, one of four ways:

1. It's not real. I don't believe it. If you can't find the source, I'm not interested.
2. I'm perfect. I don't need to change or add anything. It doesn't refer to me at all.
3. Why do people keep pressuring me? I'm quite overwhelmed as it is. I think I'll stick with the basics, and I'm content with that.
4. Am I hurt because the Prophet صَلَّى ٱللّٰهُ عَلَيْهِ وَسَلَّمَ is hurt we aren't following his sunnah? Does this story affect me and encourage/motivate/inspire me to change? Am I willing to look at my life (just my life, not anyone else) and take a deep and honest look at what I am doing, both internally and externally?

Before you automatically decide which category you fall into, sincerely look into your life, and examine with thought. I say this because this story affected me, and became a catalyst for change since it's encouraging self-examination. I remind myself of this dream when I feel down, when I don't feel like doing something, when the demon is telling me, "You don't need to do 'extras'". People are forgetful, and renewing your intention daily, for all activities means you are a mindful person working through the day with plans, ideas, and purpose. And what is your purpose as a Muslim? What do you consider to be at the top of that priority list?

Our intention (linked to purpose) is fundamental because it demonstrates the sincerity of our heart. We can be rewarded for a good action even if we aren't able to accomplish it. Be heedful of your intent, and revisit this daily. It should start with:

1. For the sake of Allah Subhanahu Wa Ta'ala. To earn His Pleasure.
2. To grasp the deen/knowledge as a means of guidance: develop my connection with Allah, and improve the condition of my heart.
3. Enhance the internal: self-analyse therefore evolve.
4. Enhance the external: sincerely spread good/positivity/deen through words and actions.

Think about the following sunnahs to put into practice if you haven't already (and when you're ready to look into others as well) ...

1. Use a miswaak/sewak (there are other times too, these are just a few).

    a. As part of wudhu.

    b. Before each prayer (salaah).

    c. Before reciting the Qur'an.

2. Recite du'a for eating.

    a. Express gratitude to Allah for the food. (Praise be to Allah.)

    b. Sit on the floor to eat.

    c. Eat and drink with the right hand.

    d. Do not find fault with the food (this is a huge one, especially in a family setting, as complaining can be a source of distress for the chef).

    e. Express gratitude to the chef.

3. Fast once/twice a week on a Monday and/ or Thursday. (There are other times too. But consistent acts are beneficial – demonstrating your commitment. Winter months make it easy, maybe even the days you work from home. If we convince ourselves it's easy/not too bad/long then we'll do it. But remember intention is important, and it should be to attain the pleasure of Allah Azza Wa Jal, being an obedient servant, and following the Prophet صَلَّى ٱللَّهُ عَلَيْهِ وَسَلَّمَ sunnah.)

4. Do wudhu before sleeping. (Also pray du'as after performing every wudhu: the shahadah, Durood Shareef, and Ayutul Kursi. There are many benefits and rewards for praying this – do a little research of your own.)

a. This is a good opportunity to perform Salaatul Tawbah before bed – "It's only two Rakaats/Rak'ahs, and I might as well since I have wudhu!" (Do you see what I mean about convincing yourself?) You could pray this salaah at any time during the day, but the night is ending the day on a good note: submission, mindfulness, and asking for forgiveness. We do make mistakes during the day. For example: could be something we saw, said, did, or ate, intentionally or absentmindedly.

b. Wear clean clothes.

c. Dust the bed three times before getting in.

d. Pray the du'as. Including Durood Shareef, Ayatul Kursi, and the last two ayahs of Surah Baqarah: 285-286 … (there are other du'as but it's just a small start to get you started).

e. Empty the heart of any malice/hate towards anyone.

There are many other sunnahs you could look into and put into practice, and pass on to others using a delicate, timely approach. I know we say we'll get to it (eventually), but if you're putting something off that you could easily add to your routine, have you asked yourself what's stopping you from actioning this act? Is it just a sunnah – or an act you deem as important because of your love for Allah and the Prophet صَلَّى ٱللَّهُ عَلَيْهِ وَسَلَّمَ ؟

Connecting with Islam, with the stories of the Prophets, and learning about their lives I've found has been the transformative self-altering factor (but of course, nothing is possible without Allah, the Guide). Connecting evolved from hedonism with little thought (which turned out to never actually be connecting, but an emptiness due to my broken heart and a distorted mental image of Self/life/others) to connecting with deeper meaning, purpose, and boundaries (with the people around me). This link was the gateway to opening the doors of bountiful possibilities, to healing and letting go. Contentment/hope would never have been possible without faith, without Allah Subhanahu Wa Ta'ala, the One Who Suffices for Everything and Everyone.

Now, when I have a pinch (i.e. emotion/memory triggered by something in my present) I can instantly feel it attacking my heart. I know some part of me wants me to go back there. It could be the demon fighting its way back from being shunned, or something internal/emotional/chemical/biological. I fight it as best as can (using these tools: prayer/dhikr, questioning the Self, exploring my feelings to understand/unpack to reach a conclusion or understand the irrationality behind a thought. And find a way of letting it go). You have to fight it too (whatever that means for you, because it means something different to each of us). Once you've determined this balanced state you will know when this attack is trying to re-emerge with force. For me, I repeat: "It is obtainable. It is obtainable. Allah is with me." What personalised mental repetition do you need? This repetition embraces immediate prayer/dhikr, and the ayahs I've mentioned in this book. A kitaab called: 'Ad Du'a,' and 'Two Priceless Treasures' have been incredibly healing (of course it is Allah Who heals) through repetition in supplication. I hope you check it out for yourself.

So how can you create a persona that believes? How can we persevere after enduring so much? What is the barrier to hope/success in your life? If you knew an invisible entity was trying to break you, trying to turn you away from your Lord by overwhelming you with hopelessness and impossibility how would you act? How would you fight it?

"Ya Allah, please help us to get closer to you. Empower us to get into action mode. Support us to fight this pain. Give us strength. Give us courage."

Our negative automatic response can be retrained. By being in a state of constant awareness of our busy minds. What are these thoughts? What do I entertain and magnify? When the pessimistic and suspiciously sarcastic 'logic' pop in I must immediately redirect.

I must counter the disapproval by being the
one to invite the encouraging energy in.
With one thought there'll be two,
and another, and another.
I am responsible for determinedly choosing
one or the other.

Positive or negative energy can overflow in me, I'm just more used to the latter, which tells me I can intently (with more conscious effort) pick positive thoughts to develop a new automatic. The emphasis is 'I CHOOSE'. We decide our future and our path once we've established successful methods/ routines that are contrary to our stagnant inaction (less phone time, less time-wasting, less useless interaction). No human being possesses the power to decide or change it for us, but us. However, with assistance from the All-Hearing, we can move ahead without fear, with determination and conviction. We are responsible for the effort. Allah is the One Who Gives Guidance He can make things fall into place.

This network of new routines (which you will need to identify on your own: these routines/ changes/habits to action) requires the spotlight one at a time. It feels impossible to achieve when you're suffering from anxiety and your mind is exploding with a plethora of unimaginable disorder. So how do you achieve new practices and routines? A step at a time. Remind yourself of the purpose, which is to live a better life. We will figure out how to fight the challenges of a mental pandemonium. In time the noise will quieten, it will get better. Do not give up this belief.

Each person's needs are specific and unique. It should make us see that Allah, the Assembler, the Self-Exalted, is capable of miracles (and all varied for each of our needs) which we are not. Providing for each of us differently, in a perfect way that is through His All-Encompassing Knowledge and Wisdom. Allah Azza Wa Jal is capable of transforming our lives in a moment. Keep in mind the bigger picture, that we are to return to our Maker who is the Most Loving, the Most Forbearing.

Pain leads to rewards in the afterlife. By being patient and grateful we can achieve success. We will, as a result, persevere. What ideas do you hold on to? "This time next year..." "This week/ project is almost over." "This contract is ending soon." "It's just another few months of this degree then I'll be done. No point quitting now." Seek help from the Most Merciful, the Remover of Difficulties, the Protector. You are not alone. "Hold firmly to the rope of Allah," this is an everlasting attachment. Allah Subhanahu Wa Ta'ala will guide, and support in the right way that we need and long for.

Do not allow that towering sarcastic undertone to take over your ability to develop and flourish.

Faith acts as an aid to make it through the journey. You won't be unscathed because it's meant to test and remodel for the better if you're receptive, willing, and Allah conscious. There is a greater understanding beyond what our minds are capable of recognising in a single moment or amidst trials. There are answers more than what our eyes can see. We cannot move forward without accepting, without accepting our past. At times accepting limitations of our bodies, our situations, and our understanding (because we evolve, grow) is a step forward.

Faith is the opening to a life beyond the agony and turmoil.

Do your best to keep the One Who Has Control Over All Things, the One Who Has the Power to Create Again, at the forefront of each day. Watch how Divine help will descend. Talk to the Most-High, the Praiseworthy each moment, and through each effort/task/obstacle/worry/pain/tribulation. Ask for all that you need, wish for, and more. Not only for yourself but others too. For example, a friend might mention she is struggling to find a new job. "Ya Allah, O the Caretaker, help my friend find the best job for her." A parent discusses the struggle with health or worrying test results which are out of our control. "Ya Allah, you are Invincible, please ease my parent's suffering and grant them relief. Grant them the best in this and every situation, through Your Wisdom."

If you don't know the Names of the Most Forbearing, try to learn one each day it will take 99 days to learn them all. Or one a week which will take roughly 22 months, or whatever works for you. Do you have a little time, like on the commute to/from work? Find and repeat one Name of Allah Ta'ala for about a week until it's sunk in.

Ar-Razzaq = the Sustainer and Provider.
Al-Kareem = the Most Generous.
Al-Mujeeb = the Answerer of Du'as.
Al-Wadood = the Most Loving.
Al-Haadi = the Guide.

Allah's Messenger صَلَّى ٱللَّهُ عَلَيْهِ وَسَلَّمَ said, "Allah has ninety-nine Names, one-hundred less one; and he who memorised them all by heart will enter Paradise." (Bukhari 7392).

The phrase, "If you come walking to Me, I will come running to you," (Bukhari 7405) tells me we are loved by our Creator. I know how much I need this reminder to keep the mocking pessimistic demon at bay so that my heart remains light, rather than heavy and cumbersome. I just keep trying, learning, and actioning. We were not made in vain, without purpose, without hope, without answers. The ultimate goal is Jannah but living in the now means finding the right balance so that even when it feels painfully agonising, you know this life is not the objective. Faith supports us to keep pushing and persevering. We can have our moments of sadness but it doesn't mean we lose our emaan or become thankless servants.

I work on the internal negative persona with positive affirmations (frequently in the form of dhikr). It is achievable once you recognise the mind is in a frenzied state and immediately convert those thoughts into something other than scrutinising torture. Don't try to battle the difficulty alone, because we belong to Allah, the Omnipresent, the Caretaker, the Benefactor.

IN CONCLUSION

What observations have you made and what do you see around you, and in you? What have you noticed in your behaviour when on your own and with company? What is your internal voice like? Are you innately positive or negative? And if so why? What are the people in your life like? Giving them the benefit of the doubt (recalling their help, love, time, gifts, words), or projecting assumptions (recalling lack of help, love, time, gifts, hurtful words)? Why do we need to do this? Because they may be having an off day, and people are capable of changing. How do you interact with them? How do you cope and navigate through difficult relationships/people and situations? What role does past hurt play in your present-day?

If you've found that this message isn't for you. I hope you find a personalised method of healing. Observe and examine yourself. Write down your own analysis. What do you recognise as failures and achievements? How do you carry on when all is lost? What comes easy to some (to keep going), doesn't come easy for others.

You are your own person, with a distinctive blend of characteristics. Therefore, choose your method of healing. Until we truly want to change and can accept that we have limitations in some areas but excel in others, then we can build on our self-analysis. We need to work on the internal out so that we aren't a cumbersome tornado of emptiness. I hope we can all aim to contribute to society, to people. Not to crumble at the sight of trouble, not to break down each time we are faced with overwhelming odds, and not to regress to thoughts that life is hopeless.

You get to write each chapter of your life, with Allah Azza Wa Jal having ultimate control. We are responsible for the action or the lack of action. It all comes down to your outlook, inner force, and consistent challenging and fighting off those pessimistic thoughts. With each trouble comes ease. Even when it feels hopeless, it will get easier. I would like to encourage you to write a list of your accomplishments. The moments in your life you are proud of, those obstacles faced and persevered. When the negativity begins its launch (but before allowing it to escalate and attack), look over what you have accomplished and overcome. Compare where you were, to where you are now. What are the privileges/gifts/favours bestowed on you by Allah Subhanahu Wa Ta'ala, the Source of Goodness, the One Who Loves Virtue and Piety?

Don't believe the comments that put you down. Don't believe the person who spreads vile deprecating nonsense. It serves you no purpose other than to underestimate. Allah is the Most-High, the Supreme, the Creator. People do not determine your success. Remember, some will admire and mean us well, whilst others will mock to weaken, regarding themselves as superior in intellect. A humble person will tell you they make mistakes, that they don't know everything. But a person with ego (uncontrolled Self)... be cautious of the company you keep. It may not surprise you that the habits and ideas of others do in some way transfer over to us if we aren't mindful. You decide your future with every step, every thought, every action. You are responsible and capable of accepting (the situation, a plan, the Self,) or not.

Allah is the Most Kind, the Most Forgiving. He is waiting for your heartfelt, all-invested (**mentally present**), emotionally honest, raw calls. We can't travel this journey alone. Allah Subhanahu Wa Ta'ala is Peace and the Giver of Peace. So long as our exploration/journey includes the Deviser at every turn we will satisfyingly reach our destination.

In order to connect with the dhikr/prayer so that we feel it inside, it must be heartfelt. (Don't sit after salaah and make du'a whilst scrolling through your phone, texting, checking/deleting emails etc.) These words must be consciously spoken by emanating from the internal. This is where the recollection of pain is an asset because it communicates with the heart. It's like the tug of an old wound that compels the awakening of exposed emotion, which only improves your connection with the Almighty. Tears are honest and humbling.

Lessons await to uplift and enrich our lives. Life-changing knowledge and wisdom in the Qur'an and the Prophet's صَلَّى ٱللّٰهُ عَلَيْهِ وَسَلَّمَ sunnah, message and life can empower, heal, and inspire. If you are willing to look beyond the surface. It requires thought, it requires internalising. There are illuminative people to connect with and still to meet on this adventure. Even new exhilarating places to visit and wander through. In time, our perspectives of an ordeal will change but the fundamental element is to uphold a level of positive persistence in our action/viewpoint/thoughts. We must persist to overcome and achieve. Be patient in the process.

Heartbreak/loss, anxiety/worry is part of every journey to educate the Self, to then connect with people (having compassion, showing mercy/kindness/patience/understanding), and excel together (encourage/remind/support one another). And return to Allah Azza Wa Jal, the Magnificent, with a pure and sincere heart. Always remember how essential it is to be thoughtful and tolerant, recalling your struggles and pain.

We may lose our way, lose our vision, and pause. But if you can come back to Allah Subhanahu Wa Ta'ala with gratitude, there is hope which can influence transformation. The Almighty's help is always near, it's just a matter of time!

Extinguish self-hatred.
Extinguish regret.
Extinguish doubt.

I pray you all gain Afiyah:
wellbeing, peace, security, serenity, happiness,
contentment, love, health, and more.
Love and peace to you all.

YA ALLAH

O The Compassionate, O The All-Powerful, O The All-Loving, O The All-Giving, O The Kind

بسم الله الرحمن الرحيم
(In the Name of Allah, the Most Compassionate, the Most Merciful)

(Recite Durood Shareef)

"There is no god worthy of worship except You. Glory be to You! I have certainly done wrong." (Surah Al-Anbiya 21:87).

O Master of the Kingdom, the Most Kind, and the Most Forgiving, forgive our shortcomings, and forgive all our mistakes, committed in secret and in public. Save us from the punishment of the grave. Save us from the Fire of Hell. Grant us mercy, clemency, protection, comfort, light, and shade on the Day of Judgement. Grant us Jannat-ul-Firdaus.

O the Benevolent, the Kind Benefactor, the

Omnipotent, praise be to Allah, for all you have given us and more. The blessings we are aware of, and the blessings we do not recognise or know of. The gifts in our past, present, and future.

O the Provider, the Answerer of Du'as, please fulfil our wishes now and forever. Give us the tools we need to achieve and carry on.

O the One Who Guides, help us to realise our purpose in life to earn Your pleasure, to seek Your guidance, and Your love. O the Compassionate, help us to improve our connection with You so that we can enrich our lives.

O the Remover of Difficulties, remove our burdens, anxieties, troubles, and tribulations. O the Overpowering Lord, the Owner of the Kingdom, the Clement, ease the strain on our hearts. Help us to let go of the past, and the obsessions/pain that prevents us from moving forward.

O the Knower of Innermost Secrets, the Subtle One, the One Who Has Control Over All things, heal our emotional, physical, and veiled wounds so that we can overcome.

O the Giver of Sustenance and Strength, the Giver of Honour, convert our pain to awareness, to contentment, to hopefulness, to courage.

O the Wise, the One Who Sees All Things, give us the ability to carry on in times of crisis and difficulty. Grant us the ability to persevere. Remind us to be grateful. Remind us to do good. Remind us to be patient.

O the Truth, the Exceedingly Forgiving, open our eyes to all things, on all fronts, on all sides. Prompt us to be more kind, merciful, calm, tolerant, and aware.

O the Most Loving, the Most Great, open our hearts to people in need of help. Open our hearts to be more considerate and compassionate, and be an encouragement by way of example to others.

O the Keeper of Counts, the Invincible, increase our love and understanding of this deen, Islam, the Qur'an, and Your beloved Prophet صَلَّى ٱللَّهُ عَلَيْهِ وَسَلَّمَ. Bestow us with guidance so that we can improve ourselves, and our hearts before we return to you.

O the Giver of Gifts, I ask you to please make our hearts, souls, and minds: clear, sound, sincere, and pure.

O the Magnificent, the Majestic and Benevolent, please lighten our load and bestow us with all that we need and more, in this life and the next.

Praise be to Allah for all that You
have given us and more.
Aameen

BIBLIOGRAPHY

Maulana Muhammed Yunus Palanpuri, *Ad Du'a Devine Help*, January 1, 2012
(Beneficial morning and evening du'as.)

Hakeem Mohammad Tariq Mahmood Majzoobi Chughtai, *Two Priceless Treasures*.

https://sunnah.com/

Critical Introspection is an analysis of the Self, exploring the chaos due to internal and external factors. The Self can be a barrier to success and progress because we can pick apart, and injure ourselves with just our thoughts (and the memories that linger from our past). These thoughts can empower/elevate or crush/deflate. Since negativity can be a wide-reaching (all-encompassing) emotion that can quickly escalate to destroying the Self, we need this self-questioning to examine the internal.

What do we entertain and magnify on an hourly, daily, regular basis?

We are capable of evolving once we understand and unravel these thoughts and emotions. When we figure out our purpose we can work on little steps of heedful action to create a better place of doing more than just surviving. Faith and belief in the One, the Creator can be a constant in our lives. We need this message of hope to keep trying and persevering. With Allah, the Most Loving, the Most Merciful Lord we can achieve and flourish.

Follow me on this journey of admission and exploration...

MORE BOOKS COMING SOON